CUCAMONGA VALLEY WINE

The LOST EMPIRE OF AMERICAN WINEMAKING

George M. Walker & John Peragine

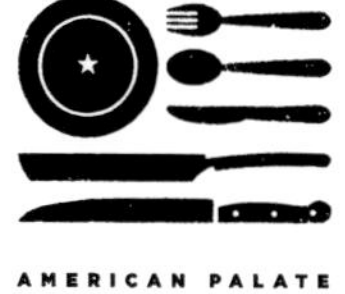

Published by American Palate
A Division of The History Press
Charleston, SC
www.historypress.net

Cover: It's harvest time at Guasti Vineyards. Mexican migrant workers fill the backs of trucks with thousands of tons of grapes to be transported back to the winery for crushing and pressing. Photo taken on October 26, 1937. *Cal Poly Collections*.

First published 2017

Manufactured in the United States

ISBN 9781625859112

Library of Congress Control Number: 2017940951

This book is dedicated to all of the families of those vineyard and winemaking pioneers named herein who were responsible for bringing the Cucamonga Valley to such great fame during a time when our country went through two world wars, the Great Depression, Prohibition and the infancy of the now famous winegrowing pedigree of the State of California. May the writing of this book help lead to new awareness of and a new appreciation for these winegrowing pioneers' struggles, hard work, foresight and passion.

CONTENTS

ACKNOWLEDGEMENTS

We would like to thank all those who made this project possible. First of all, our families—without their support, we could not spend hours drinking, making, talking and writing about wine. We call it our vocation, while others might see it as our obsession.

There are some special people we wanted to mention up front, as they not only supported this project but also provided us material, photographs and, in some cases, some very tasty food and wine: Don Galleano and his son, Dominic; the staff at Galleano Winery; the staff at Mountain Vista Winery; Pierre and Michael Biane; Katie Richardson, Alexis Adkins and the terrific staff and students at Cal Poly Pomona's Special Collections Department; and Mark and Debbie Bianco.

George Walker's son, Clayton G. Walker, would like to add:

"I am proud to play an active and integral role in the restoration of the Cucamonga Valley. Over the last ten years, my father and I have been diligently and committedly working to rescue as many remaining Cucamonga old vines as possible before they are destroyed by continuous urban development. Moreover, we have replanted various parts of Cucamonga with thousands of new vines, thanks to homeowners who have engaged us to help them attain their own vineyard dreams. Suffice it to say, MyHomeVineyard.com is passionate about the world's most notable plant—the grapevine."

INTRODUCTION TO A LOST WINEMAKING EMPIRE

The discovery of a wine is of greater moment than the discovery of a constellation. The universe is too full of stars.
—Benjamin Franklin

Today, whenever someone mentions wine in California, the first places people think of are Sonoma and the Napa Valley, as these areas not only dominate the California wine industry but also are the top producers of wine in the world, due to their vast vineyards and gigantic production facilities. This may be where the industry is today, but it is not where it started. It really began much farther south, in an area of California that was once part of Mexico.

If you enjoy American wine, it is because of the dedicated farmers and winemakers who struggled to bring life to vineyards in a desert of sand ruled by jackrabbits. If it were not for the efforts of dedicated immigrant families, wine in California and within the United States would not exist as it does today. Prohibition had all but wiped out the wine industry, except in the sandy foothills of the San Gabriel Mountains.

Mel Blanc used to mention Cucamonga often in one of his bits on *The Jack Benny Program*. There would be a scene of a train station, and Mel Blanc would voice over, "Train leaving on Track 5 for Anaheim, Azusa and Cu [pause] camonga!" There were a number of viewers who thought the place and name were made up for the show. The exception was those who knew California wine.

Within the foreground of the San Gabriel Mountains is an area that was once the very heart of the wine industry. Cucamonga, now known as Rancho Cucamonga, was at the hub of this once thriving area. If you were to drive through this area now, you would see many industrial storage facilities covering the sandy soil that once held a vast acreage of sprawling vineyards.

The current city of Rancho Cucamonga is at the western edge of San Bernardino County. It is situated along Highways 66 (the famed Route 66) and 99 and extends north to Etiwanda on the east and Alta Loma on the west, stretching south to Ontario, Guasti and the Riverside County Line. The Cucamonga Valley, which was known decades ago as the Cucamonga-Guasti Wine District, included the communities of Alta Loma, Cucamonga, Etiwanda, Grapeland, Rochester, Ontario (Guasti), Fontana, Mira Loma (formerly known as Wineville), Rialto, Upland, North Ontario and Magnolia. It was an area steep in vineyards and was known for its wines, especially such Italian varietals such as Barbera, Grignolino, Zinfandel and Chianti.

Urban sprawl, vine disease and tax values for property caused these vineyards to be bulldozed and turned into large concrete edifices, which mark inevitable growth and progress as families and businesses moved eastward through the Inland Valley. Over time, the only evidence of the vast acres of grapevines are only a few hundred remaining acres of vines, historical markers and artwork integrated into street signs, as well as the architecture of some of buildings. If passersby look closely, they may also see a small vineyard planted in front of a home or in the courtyard of a business. These few relics pale in comparison to the scale of the twenty thousand contiguous acres that were once full of grapes of various varietals.

The once-thriving winegrowing industry in this area is important in a larger historical sense. Even during the Prohibition era, the area flourished economically, growing grapes and still legally making sacramental and prescription wine under federal permit, while other wineries and vineyards nationwide were abandoned or closed. Because Cucamonga continued to grow and even expand vineyards during this time, when the Volstead Act was finally repealed in 1933, the vineyards and local winemaking thrived and became the foundation of the new wine industry in California, not to mention the nation.

The area was a melting pot of different cultures and immigrants from all over the world, and this helped to make the grapes grown and the wines they produced legendary. Some of these vineyards still exist, although on a

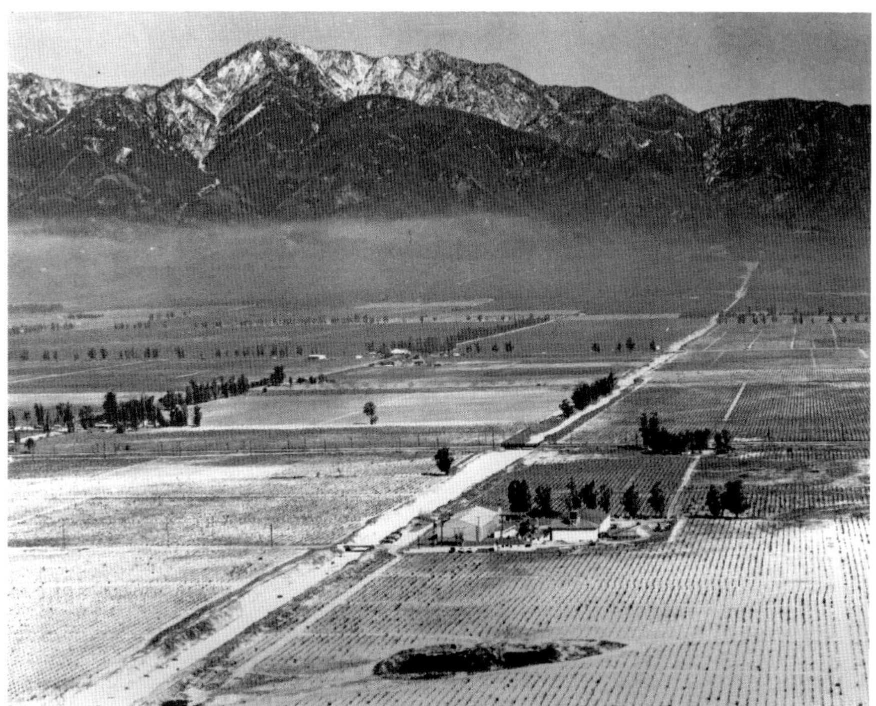

Day Creek Channel on West Seventh Street, south of Cucamonga Winery. *Cal Poly Special Collections.*

much smaller scale, and some are still farmed by the descendants of a few of those original families. With the continued urban sprawl and property values increasing, the next generation's interest (or lack of interest) in taking over the family vineyard/winery business placed the future of these historic vineyards and wineries in a highly unsure light.

Chapter 1

MISSION WINE

The story of winegrowing in California begins in 1525 with Hernán Cortéz, who was at the time the governor of Mexico. He ordered the planting of grapes for producing wine, but by 1595, the king of Spain was worried that the colony would become too independent in its wine production. So, the king forbade new plantings of grapes or new vineyards, and his ruling on this subject effectively prevented commercial wine production for more than 150 years.

In the eighteenth century, Spain was again interested in exploring more of North America. In 1769, a group of soldiers was led into Baja California by Captain Gaspar de Portolà. With him was a group of Franciscan monks led by Father Junípero Serra, who had hopes of colonizing and bringing Christianity to the area. Father Serra (now Saint Serra) developed a mission system of ranchos, which were to be used for cattle production using a type of feudal system.

In 1774, Captain Juan Bautista de Anza was searching for an overland route to California. He came upon a desert region while making his way along the Mission Road to San Gabriel. He found a Native American village the locals called Cucamongabit, "Place of Many Springs." When he reached the San Gabriel Mission, he reported finding the village to Friar Jose Maria Talvida. The land was desirable because it lies between the area known as Los Angeles and San Bernardino. He described the land as gently sloping northward into the mountains in a "wild waste of rocks, cactus, plumbush, manzanita, and sagebrush." There were some creeks in the area, and it seemed to be the perfect place to establish a village. Friar Jose gave the area the name "Nuestra Senora del Pilar de Cucamonga." A number of ranches were built on the Mission Road to provide places for travelers to stop on their journey through desert and plains.

The first vineyard was planted by Father Junípero Serra at the mission in San Diego. Eight more missions and supporting vineyards were built in California before his death in 1784. These particular grapes became known as "Mission grapes" and were the standard grape used in winemaking until about 1880. The wines produced were particularly used for sacramental purposes and for selling/trading to help finance the missions. In about 1830, the missions were secularized, and a new economy of winemaking was born in California. In addition to wine, brandy was also produced in the missions.

European vines were first planted in the Los Angeles area in 1833 by Jean-Louis Vignes (which, incidentally, is the French word for "vines"). Vignes owned and operated his vineyard and winery until 1885, at which time his nephews took over and continued the operation into the 1890s. Vignes was from the Bordeaux region in France, and although it was rumored that he introduced Cabernet Sauvignon, Merlot, Sauvignon Blanc and Semillon, there is no documentation to confirm this.

Another important person from this period of winemaking in California was William Wolfskill. Even though he arrived in Los Angeles around the same time as Vignes, he differed dramatically in that he was not born into the culture of winemaking. Wolfskill was from Kentucky, and he was looking to make his fortune in California, so he bought land already planted with grapevines. Before his death in 1886, Wolfskill created 145 acres of vineyards and orchards, and his winery was producing up to fifty thousand gallons of wine per year.

The first vineyards in Cucamonga began being planted around 1839. Other areas east of Los Angeles began growing grapes as well. In La Puente, William Workman and John Rowland planted vineyards in the 1840s. In Rancho Santa Anita, Hugo Reid planted a vineyard in 1839 where a certain famed racetrack and an arboretum now stand. By 1850, there were about one hundred vineyards in and around Los Angeles. The wines produced from these vines were sold for fifteen cents per gallon.

The gold rush in California began in 1848 when James W. Marshall found gold at Sutter's Mill in Coloma, California, with the rush lasting until 1855. While San Francisco grew due to the gold rush, Southern California was not as directly affected. What did grow in Southern California was the demand for wine to be sent north in large quantities. So, the vineyards in the region grew. The nephews who took over for Vignes, the Sainsevain brothers, opened a store in San Francisco in 1857 to sell the wines that they produced in Southern California.

In 1875, the Southern Pacific Railroad was completed, and it connected San Bernardino and San Gabriel. A station was established in the Cucamonga Valley in order to haul mail and freight to the California Fruit Lands Company in the southern part of Cucamonga. The area grew and a water tower was built, along with a house near the railroad and a hotel. In 1877, a fire, with the assistance of the Santa Ana winds, destroyed the little town that had been built. The community was rebuilt even larger than before with a new hotel, livery stable and telegraph office. The rail line eventually became the Union Pacific line.

Anaheim

This boom in winemaking led to wine development in Anaheim, which at the time was part of Los Angeles County. The area was developed by two German musicians, John Frohling and Charles Kohler. They had come to San Francisco to make it big in the winegrowing industry. They started by producing wines in the Los Angeles area to sell in what was a very busy and growing San Francisco.

Kohler and Frohling saw an opportunity to expand, so they developed a winegrowing colony. There was interest from German investors in San Francisco, so these investors bought shares in the Los Angeles Vineyard Society. Land was purchased along the Santa Ana River to begin the colony. The ten thousand acres that were planned to host the potential vineyard were split up into smaller lots. A massive irrigation system was then built, and 400,000 vines were planted. It took two years of preparation, and in 1859, the first members of the colony arrived. The first year's harvest produced only 2,000 gallons, but the vines were still young, and more colony members were on their way. Over the next twenty years, the colony grew to more than fifty wineries, which collectively produced more than 1 million gallons of wine.

In 1856, in the San Gabriel Valley, Benjamin Wilson began making wine at his Lake Vineyard estate. Up to this time, the Mission grape was still dominant, but Wilson added Carignane, Zinfandel, Grenache,

Mataro (Mourvedre), Trousseau, Burger and Folle Blanche to the list of grape varietals grown. He is also credited for making the first California sparkling wine in 1856.

By 1867, Wilson had increased the storage capacity of Lake Vineyard to fifty thousand gallons, and at this time, his son-in-law, J. DeBarth Shorb, began helping with the business. Over the next fifteen years, the business grew with the hopes of becoming the largest winery in the world. This growth was occurring during the tremendous disaster that hit European vineyards: phylloxera, a tiny insect that decimated most vineyards in Europe and all but destroyed the European wine market.

The root louse, *Phylloxera vastatrix*, actually originated in North America. Some native vines were brought back to botanical gardens in England by avid English botanists, but no one knew they carried the insect, and no one knew what that insect could do. The insect attacks the vine roots and leaves of grapevines and was primarily found in the Mississippi Valley. Until 1863, it had not been seen outside North America. Because of that, no one knew how destructive and widespread phylloxera would become.

As the pest lived in North America, the native grapevines had developed a resistance to phylloxera, so they were all but immune to the pest. Because phylloxera had never encountered European *vinifera*, though, they had no natural defense against it. They caused girdling of the roots, which resulted in the vines being deprived of nutrients and water. After quickly feeding on one vine, the insects then go on to feed on the next. Consequently, in only two short years, the pests had made their way from England to the grapevines in Provence, and over the next twenty years, they almost completely decimated vineyards across Europe. Of course, if the European wine market was to survive, something had to be done.

All sorts of treatments, such as flooding and injecting the soil with carbon bisulfide, were attempted (some even planted live toads at the vine roots), and while these treatments (with the exception of the toads) stopped the louse for short periods, the methods were costly. Once a treatment ended, the pests simply returned.

In Dennison, Texas, a horticulturist, Thomas Munson, came up with a solution that changed grape growing in a profound way that is still widely used today. He grafted the *vinifera* vines with *ripara* (native vines) hybrid rootstocks. The grapes that were produced were still the *vinifera* grapes, but now the roots had a resistance to phylloxera. The solution was a success, and every wine vine in Europe was then grafted with the American rootstock. Unfortunately, some indigenous European grapevines became extinct because they did not have a commercial value and, therefore, were not grafted—phylloxera destroyed them all.

Some believed that the fruit of the new grafted vines resulted in the production of inferior wines. No one was sure whether it was due to the American rootstock, the fact that the newly grafted vines were all young or that there were new growing techniques being used. Still, during this period, the wine industry was in shambles, and there was a lot of wine fraud and adulteration occurring. French winemakers wanted to protect their interests and formed the Appellation Contrôlée. This became the model for all wine-producing countries in order to authenticate grape growing and wine production for consumers while protecting the reputations of the participating wine regions.

During this period, it was thought that the European wine industry would not recover. The European disaster created an opportunity for winemakers across the United States, and especially in Southern California, to increase their share of the world market. By 1900, the wine industry in America was flourishing, and its reputation for producing quality wines was increasing. Even wine lists in the finest restaurants were including American wines alongside their European counterparts.

Close to Lake Vineyard, L.J. Rose and neighbor Lucky Baldwin opened a 500,000-gallon winery called Sunny Slope. They produced a variety of wines and brandy from their 1,200-acre vineyard.

All signs pointed toward Anaheim and surrounding areas becoming the dominant winemaking center of California, if not the world. In 1883, Anaheim had its own crisis, as its vines began withering from some unknown disease. In 1884, even more vines died, and it became known as the Anaheim disease. In was not until later in 1892 that Newton B. Pierce (1856–1916), California's first professional plant pathologist, identified Anaheim disease as resulting from a bacterial infection, spread by a leaf-hopper insect. It was then named "Pierce's disease."

Pierce's disease is caused by bacteria, which is spread by the glassy-winged sharpshooter (GWSS). This is a leaf-hopping insect that spreads the disease quickly by feeding on the vine shoots. Even today, with all the scientific marvels for effectively treating diseases, there is no cure. Once introduced into the vine's xylem via the feeding GWSS, the bacteria create a gel-like substance that prevents water from traveling through the vine, which chokes and withers. The bacteria continue to infect all of the vine over a period of one to five years, and the entire vine eventually dies. The GWSS stay in areas that are wet and near rivers, and they live extensively in citrus, oleander, eucalyptus and other trees and plants. Following the loss of all the vines in the Anaheim area, landowners turned to cultivating citrus, and soon the area was called "Orange County" rather than "Grape County."

Vineyard owners ripped out the vineyards and began planting oranges and other citrus because they were immune to the disease. Southern California became the heart of the citrus industry in the United States. This was prior to citrus growing in places such as Florida and Texas. Eventually, the citrus industry began eroding for much the same reason that the wine industry did: urbanization. It was hard for farmers to sell their land to other farmers for $8,000 per acre when they could get $100,000 per acre from industrial developers.

During the period when California turned toward citrus, Cucamonga held out. While it did plant a number of citrus groves, Cucamonga continued to expand its vineyards. Cucamonga's soil was primarily sandy, which meant that vines grown there were immune to phylloxera, as it does not thrive in sandy, well-drained soils. At the time, it was not a breeding ground for the GWSS, so Pierce's disease was not a problem. While the soil was very sandy, water also ran deep beneath the surface. The vines' natural tap root enabled the Cucamonga vines to grow in an otherwise barren terrain, as the tap roots would run deep enough to find moisture in the ground, continuing to travel deeper with each ensuing year. This also meant that the vineyards could be "dry-farmed," meaning that the vines needed irrigation only for the first few years after planting to get the vines started.

CUCAMONGA RANCHO

There was a great deal of expansion in California during the nineteenth century. By 1833, Spain had lost its control over what is Southern California and Baja California and Mexico had won its independence. The Mexican governor, Juan Bautista Alvarado, began giving land grants. Tuberio Tapia—who was a soldier, politician and known smuggler—was granted thirteen thousand acres of land known as Cucamonga on March 3, 1839. Tapia used local indigenous laborers and built an adobe home on Red Hill in the city now known as Rancho Cucamonga.

In addition to raising cattle, Tapia planted hundreds of acres of vineyards and built a winery that is recognized as California's oldest winery and the second oldest in the United States. Tapia hired Jose Valdez to help him to build his home and plant his vineyard; 564 Mission grapevines were planted. Over twenty years, 250,000 vines were planted, and the ranch became known as Thomas Winery. Today portions of the original facility still exist and have been preserved through adaptive reuse. The old structure is now home to a sports bar, a coffeehouse and a small winery.

John Rains

California was invaded by American soldiers in 1846, and by 1848, it had been annexed. Finally, in 1850, it was ratified as a state. In 1858, cattle rancher John Rains and his wife, Maria Merced Williams de Rains, bought Cucamonga Rancho from Tapia's daughter and her husband, Leon Victor Prudhomme. Rains expanded the vineyards, which had been started by Tapia, to 125,000 vines, and he constructed his brick home, which still stands and is listed in the National Register of Historic Places. Rains introduced agriculture on a large scale and began to replace traditional cattle and sheep raising in the region.

Unfortunately, Rains had overextended his finances, and on November 17, 1862, he planned to head to Los Angeles to sign the papers for a mortgage on the rancho. During those days, it was not particularly safe to travel long distances alone, especially without some armed protection. While it was normal for Rains to be armed, when he looked for his guns on that fateful day, they seemed to be missing.

As the story goes, Rains hitched his horses and traveled by wagon. After two days, his team of horses returned, but there was no wagon and no John Rains. Oddly, no one called the authorities to report that Rains was missing. A few days after Rains went missing, the men he was supposed to meet in Los Angeles arrived at the rancho to inquire where Rains was, as he had never arrived for his appointment. This is when the search commenced.

A posse of men was rounded up by the sheriff of Los Angeles County. First, they found Rains's wagon in the Mud Springs near San Dimas. The harness for the horses was found in a tree, and lying on the ground was Rain's bloodstained hat and overcoat. The worst was assumed.

Finally, eleven days after John Rains had left his home, his body was found in a cactus patch near Azusa, which is just a few miles west of where his wagon was found. He had been brutally murdered. On November 29, 1862, the *Los Angeles Star* printed the following:

> *Yesterday, the body of Mr. Rains was discovered. It was lying about four hundred yards from the main road, in a cactus patch. The body gave evidence that the unfortunate gentleman had been lassoed, dragged from his wagon by the right arm, which was torn from the socket, and the flesh mangled from the elbow to the wrist. He had been shot twice in the back, also in the left breast, and in right side. His clothes were torn off him, and he lost one boot in the struggle. The body was not far from where the wagon was concealed.*
>
> *The funeral will take place tomorrow* [Sunday] *evening at 10 o'clock at the Bella Union Hotel. Friends are respectfully invited to attend.*

Rains's brother-in-law, Robert Carlisle, who had joined the search for Rains, was determined to locate his killer. There was the question of the missing pistols and the fact that no alarm was raised when his horses had returned on their own. This pointed to someone at the rancho being part of the murder plot. There were rumors that his wife, Merced, may even have been part of the conspiracy—if not actively, then she at least knew something of it.

The Mountain View House, a local inn not far from Rains's home, was run by William Rubottom, a friend to John and Merced Rains. One night, a group of twelve people who had been loyal friends to John Rains came in to have dinner and a serious discussion. They were heavily armed and were set on going to the Rains ranch and lynching the mistress of the rancho. Rubottom and his son-in-law armed themselves in the next room in order to stop the men from executing their plan. Rubottom did not believe that hanging a woman without a fair trial was justice.

Rubottom pointed his double-barreled shotgun at the men, who were still eating, and informed them there would be no lynching. His son-in-law disarmed the men without incident, and the men left with instructions that they could return one at a time to reclaim their guns. Fortunately, after that incident, there were no further threats on Rains's widow's life.

There were a number of people accused of the murder, but no one was ever convicted. One of those men, Manuel Corradel, gave testimony in court that he and some other men were the ones who killed Rains. In his testimony, he described how Rains drew his gun in self-defense and shot Corradel. He also testified that Ramon Carrillo, the stock foreman of the ranch hand, was an accomplice. Carrillo, however, had a solid alibi.

In Corradel's testimony, he mentioned that Rains shot him with a gun, but he described it as a small derringer, which was different than Rains's usual pistol sidearms. This further suggested that someone in the household was likely an accomplice. Even though Corradel claimed to have killed Rains, he was not convicted due to the implausibility of his story.

There are a few theories about why Rains was killed. Although he was known for having a temper, he did not have any obvious enemies. One theory states that his killing was a case of mistaken identity. Many of the surrounding ranchos were held by Californios and their families, but American banks and investors held the mortgages. One of those ranchos belonged to Hyman Tischler. He had foreclosed on Rancho San Jose, and the tenants were not happy about the situation. Tischler and a colleague were traveling from Rancho San Jose at about the same time Rains was killed. Rancho San Jose was situated next to Cucamonga Rancho and was on Tischler's way to San Bernardino. While traveling, Tischler's colleague, Edward Newman, was shot by someone hiding in the bushes.

It was believed by Tischler that Newman was not the intended target, but rather Robert Carlisle. The theory was that if Carlisle was a target, Rains could have been as well. Tempers ran high within the Mexican community that Rains and Carlisle had gained huge portions of land through marriages to Maria Merced and her sister, Francisca Williams.

Carlisle became the power of attorney for the estate, which created problems between him and Ramon Carrillo. Carlisle wanted to run the estate the way he saw fit, and Carrillo often stood in the way. Carrillo had an untimely demise, being shot from his horse while riding near Merced Rains, who was in her carriage. Once again, Merced was in the middle of a controversy—many felt that Merced was guilty of Carrillo's death because she was the last one to see Carrillo alive, and many people still believed she had some part in her husband's murder as well. Carrillo crawled away from where he was shot and died at Rubottom's inn. Like Rains's murder, there was a list of potential suspects of who killed Carrillo, but no one was ever brought to justice.

Andrew King was the receiver of the ranch, and Robert Carlisle was very vocal in his disapproval of him. On July 5, 1865, the wedding of Caroline Newmark and Solomon Lazard took place at the Bella Union Hotel, of which John Rains had once been a co-owner. Robert Carlisle and his wife, Francesca, attended the wedding. Carlisle and King got into an argument in the lobby of the hotel, but King did not want to cause a scene at the wedding. Suddenly, one of Carlisle's friends grabbed King, and then another stabbed him. King drew his revolver and tried to shoot Carlisle but missed. Others jumped in and stopped the fight from escalating any further.

The next day, the brothers of Andrew King—Frank and Houston—saw Carlisle inside the bar at the Bella Union Hotel. They entered with their guns drawn. Carlisle, upon seeing the men, drew his gun, and a gunfight ensued. Carlisle shot and killed Frank King. Houston King shot Carlisle a number of times, and Carlisle fell to the floor. Before he died, however, he got up, braced himself against the wall and shot Houston King. But Houston King survived. Carlisle died on a billiard table in the hotel bar a few hours later. King was acquitted of the killing, and a new law was passed that forbade the carrying of firearms indiscriminately within Los Angeles city limits. Francesca Carlisle later married Dr. F. McDougall, who eventually became the mayor of Los Angeles.

Later that year, Cucamonga Rancho fell deeper into debt. Merced borrowed $5,000 as a second mortgage on the property, but it was not enough to save the rancho, which went into foreclosure. In 1870, it was sold to a group of land developers that later created the Cucamonga Land Company. In 1871, Isaias W. Hellman bought a large portion of the Cucamonga Rancho for $49,000.

Merced later remarried to Jose C. Carrillo, who was a relative of the murdered Ramon Carrillo. She moved near Los Angeles with her daughter, Francisca, and her son-in-law, Henry T. Gage. Gage went on to be the twentieth governor of California.

Hellman sold off a few thousand acres but then created a consortium with Governor John Downey, O.W. Childs and his cousin Isaiah M. Hellman. They subdivided the remaining land to be used for agricultural purposes. Hellman kept the vineyards started by Rains and Tapia and employed Jean-Louis Sainsevain, a winemaker, to restore and expand the vineyards.

Sainsevain was a carpenter from the Bordeaux region of France and in 1839 came to California. His mission was to find his uncle, Jean-Louis Vignes, in Los Angeles. He located his uncle on his estate, El Aliso, and he helped in the fruit tree orchards and with winemaking.

Sainsevain was granted Rancho del Rincon en el Rio San Lorenzo near Santa Cruz, California, by Governor Manuel Micheltorena. In the fall of 1843, he built a sawmill in the San Lorenzo River Valley. He continued to build his businesses by constructing a flour mill on the Guadalupe River in San Jose. In 1845, Sainsevain married into the Sunol family, who owned Rancho Los Coches.

In 1859, Sainsevain sold Rancho Cañada del Rincon en el Rio San Lorenzo, and with the money and the help of his brother, Jean Louis, he bought the El Aliso vineyards in Los Angeles from their uncle, Jean-

Louis Vignes. The brothers decided to expand the vineyard, and in 1857, they opened a store in San Francisco. By 1858, they were producing 125,000 gallons of wine and brandy, and in their San Francisco cellars, they produced champagne. The expansion into sparkling wine was not a success, and soon the winery began suffering financial losses. The brothers dissolved their partnership, but Jean Louis remained at the El Aliso property until it was sold in 1865.

In 1870, the Sainsevain brothers moved to Cucamonga and ran the vineyard and winery with Joseph S. Garcia. The Sainsevain vineyard planted another forty thousand vines and began making port, brandy and Angelica. The vineyard, for a time, was the largest in the state of California. Sainsevain moved to Central America in 1875 and eventually returned to his home in San Jose. After his wife died in 1883, Sainsevain returned to France to live out his days.

Chapter 2

SECONDO GUASTI

FATHER OF WINE IN CUCAMONGA

Secondo Guasti is considered the founder of the expansive wine industry in Cucamonga. He landed in California in Los Angeles in 1883, and he possessed only one American dollar. Fortune shone on Guasti, and he was able to grow that one dollar into the foundations of an enormous wine empire. In 1900, Guasti, an immigrant from Italy's Piedmont region, founded the Italian Vineyard Company. He stated that he made the desert bloom as the rose, as he had created vineyards where apparently there was no water. He bought a large expanse of land near what is now Ontario, California, but back then, they were large desert tracts on which water could be run, but with great difficulty—if water could be found at all. Guasti recognized the type of soil, as it was the same he was used to cultivating back in the foothills of Italy. He knew that there was water deep below the surface and that if the right kind of vines were planted, their roots could run deep to tap into that water. He sold shares of the land to those wanting to plant vineyards, and they cultivated five thousand acres of land prior to Prohibition.

Secondo was used to hard work and enterprise. His father, Javanne Guasti, owned a grocery store, bakery and winery in their native village in Italy and worked there until he died at the age of fifty-four. Secondo was born in Prince Monto, Mombaruzzo, in the province of Alessandria, Italy, on May 29, 1859, near the town of Asti in the Piedmont region of Northern Italy. Secondo's mother, Magdelena Guasti, lived and died in Prince Monto. Secondo had a brother and two sisters. The boys went on to California, while their sisters stayed in Italy and were married.

As Secondo grew up, he helped his father to cultivate grapes and learned how to manufacture wine. He also learned baking and cooking from helping in his father's bakery. Secondo was a very studious child and often dreamed of what it might be like to live in America. He read all that he could about America. In 1881, Secondo traveled to Panama, South America, to help in the construction of a canal by the French across the isthmus. He was a very focused and determined young man.

He arrived in Panama and sought to find and work for the famous French engineer De Lesseps. What Secondo found when he arrived was an epidemic of yellow fever, which had infected about four hundred people at the site. The Italian consul encouraged Guasti not to stay and recommended that he book passage to San Francisco immediately. He arrived in America on July 3, 1881, and there was a lot of activity and talk going on about the assassination of President Garfield.

Guasti had arrived with very little money and no friends. He booked a room at a little Italian hotel on Montgomery Street, the Roma Hotel. He mentioned that he could cook, as he had learned from his father, and inquired if the hotel needed a second cook. The manager of the hotel laughed and said to Guasti that if he could cook well enough to be a second cook in Italy, he could be the first cook in San Francisco. He was hired on the spot. Guasti had brought a little Italian cookbook with him and began studying it at night when he was not working to prepare for dishes they would cook the next day.

Guasti began saving his money and soon had enough capital to begin thinking about and planning his future. In 1882, Guasti traveled to Guaymas, Mexico, and went into business with a few other Italians to open a restaurant. He and his partners were very successful. At the time, the Santa Fe Railway was building a line from Guaymas to Benson, Arizona. Guasti and his partners secured a contract to provide food for the construction workers, and this venture proved to be an even bigger success for the men.

Yellow fever broke out in the area, and Guasti decided to cross back over the border, landing in Tucson, Arizona. Unfortunately, Guasti himself caught yellow fever and was sick for many months. Once he recovered, he decided to move to Los Angeles on November 3, 1883. He was accompanied by one of his restaurant partners, Achille Bartalle. Guasti had arrived with only one dollar, as the rest of the fortune from Mexico was gone.

Guasti went back to working as a cook in a restaurant, again saving his money with the intention of going back into business for himself. He was able to save enough to buy the Italian Hotel on Alameda Street. He grew his business and, within a few years, was able to construct his own winery.

Guasti had developed a reputation as an excellent cook, and soon after working as a cook in Los Angeles, he made the acquaintance of Giuseppi Anillo, an Italian grocer. One day, Anillo's wife, Catherine Benaro Anillo, came into the restaurant and asked Guasti to prepare spaghetti the way they cooked it back in Italy. Guasti, in a joking manner, told Mrs. Anillo that he would be glad to prepare the dish for her, but the payment would be the hand of her daughter in marriage. Mrs. Anillo, knowing he was joking, agreed to the deal. At the time, her daughter was just a young girl, but the promise had become a prophecy.

As Louisa Amillo grew up, she worked for Guasti as a secretary and bookkeeper. Guasti was taken by her, and so he wooed and married her on August 23, 1886. Amillo continued to run his office for sixteen years as Guasti continued to explore the winery business.

Guasti started the Guasti Winery in Los Angeles and used grapes he grew on the property. He acquired and ran the Barnard Winery, which was on Second and Alameda Streets, and continued his own winery business for ten years. In 1889, Guasti moved Guasti Winery from his Aliso Street location to Palmetto Street. In 1897, he rented and ran the Glendale Winery for many years.

He became discontented with his five-thousand-gallon wine business and looked to the east. The patch of land referred to as the "Cucamonga Desert" was appealing to him. He had memories of vineyards in Italy that were planted in soil that did not look fertile and in areas where other plants would not grow. He remembered vineyards planted in rugged, unclad mountains that looked very much like Cucamonga. The vines thrived even without irrigation. The secret was the rich, moist loam beneath the surface that was made from pulverized granite that had washed down the mountains for centuries.

At the time, there was one house in the desert area, and no one lived there. The sandstorms were so bad that at times the Southern Pacific railroad line that ran through the area was blocked by sand that obscured the tracks. When Guasti first suggested planting vineyards in the arid area, neighbors and other people who knew the area laughed at him. He would not be dissuaded.

Guasti saw some small vineyards had already been planted on the periphery of the desert, and he approached these farmers with the idea of turning the desert into large tracts of vineyards. One of the farmers responded, "Oh, pshaw! Give your money to charity if you're bound to get rid of it, and spend the time throwing horseshoes. Just one fine old sandstorm out yonder will bury your labors forever."

Guasti got on his hands and knees and dug into the soil in different places to find the loam like there was in Italy, and he found it. Guasti was encouraged, and he believed that it would be money, not water, that was needed to make the land workable as a profitable vineyard. He could use the money to confound the devastating sandstorms. He dreamed of building the world's largest vineyards in one of the most inhospitable places on the planet.

ANTONIO SIGNORIO

In 1895, an Italian immigrant, Antonio Signorio, met an immigrant from France, Mr. Pellesiers, while living in Santa Barbara, and both of them had a love for wine and winemaking. Signorio had been experimenting with grape growing in the Asti region in north California. Mr. Pellesiers owned a tract of land in the Cucamonga Valley. Mr. Pellesiers believed that the land was fertile enough to grow grapes, and so they struck a partnership to begin a vineyard there. They planted vines in an area that became Chaffey College, but their experiment was a failure. They had planted in a severe drought period, and after four years, the vines dried up and the fruit failed. The men lost the land, and Antonio returned to Santa Barbara, but he had not given up the notion that planting vines could work in the Cucamonga Valley.

Guasti set out to find the investors and capital he needed to make his dream a reality. Guasti had heard of Antonio and sent for him. Antonio told him that he believed that the soil was fertile enough to grow grapes. He pointed out that because there had been a severe drought, the land was cheap in the valley. Guasti brought potential investors into the desert and dug with his hands to show them the loam that existed beneath, but many people could not see beyond the desert that was before them.

In the early 1880s, there had been some attempts to develop the area, but the results were disastrous. Only one ranch house stood near the railroad tracks, long abandoned. There was a boom in the 1880s, and the land had been staked off for development, as it was once thought of as a perfect place to build a resort. The stakes remained to mark off property lines and avenues, but nothing else stood. The plan had been a bust. The sand was seven inches deep, but there was fertile soil beneath it. Guasti was not a foolish businessman; he had a soil scientist at the state university

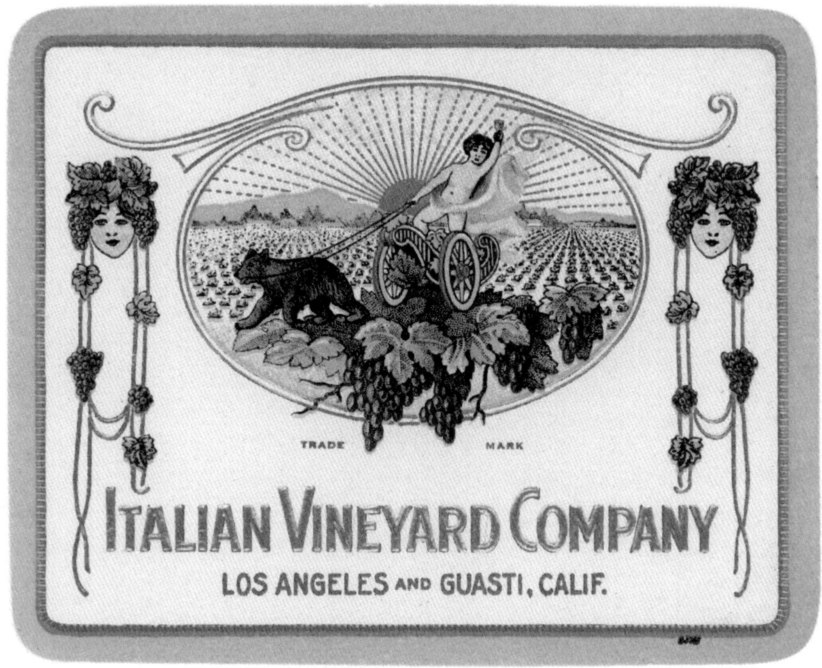

A wine bottle label from the Italian Vineyard Company. *Cal Poly Special Collections.*

in Berkeley analyze the soil before they began the venture. The scientist confirmed Guasti's theory that the soil was fertile beneath and perfect for growing grapevines.

As Guasti began bringing on potential investors, he had some difficulty finding the owners of the parcels of land, and so the process was slowed down further.

The Italian Vineyard Company

Eventually, Guasti and his investors created the Italian Vineyard Company on October 4, 1900. Guasti was the president and J.A. Barlotti the secretary. Other investors included Ambrigio Vignolo, Giovanni Gai, Angelo Bessolo and Joe Pagliano. The first incorporation of the Italian Vineyard Company had raised $500,000, and they used this to buy an additional two thousand acres (for about $15 to $35 per acre) and plant grapes on four thousand acres in San Bernardino County. This became known as the Guasti Vineyard.

It was not without its challenges. First, there were the windstorms that Guasti had been warned about. When men came to begin to prepare the land for plantings, they were blinded by a windstorm and lost their way, ending up in a town twelves miles out of their way.

The second challenge was the wildlife that held dominion over the area, namely jackrabbits. There were large-scale jackrabbit drives to get them to leave the land. It took sixty-five mule teams to clear the land, and twenty-six varieties of grapes were planted. They were not, however, successful in keeping the animals out, and after the vineyard was finished, a $4,000 rabbit fence had to be erected, as the grapevines provided a tasty treat for the jackrabbits.

Guasti enlisted the assistance of the Italian consul in Los Angeles and encouraged Italian immigrants to come to the Cucamonga Valley with the promise of permanent work.

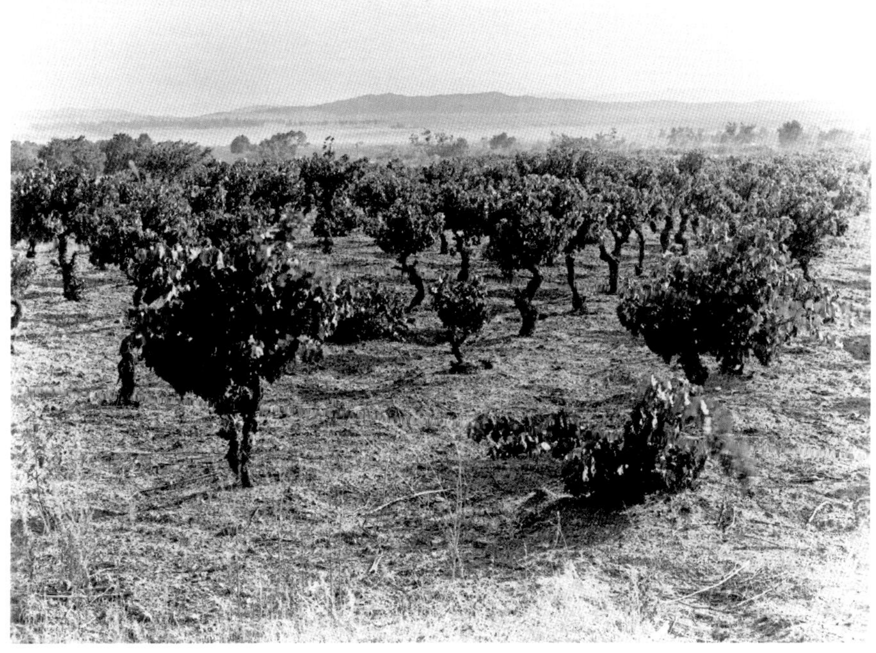

Vineyard with head-pruned vines (no stakes). Sand shifting from the north wind can also be seen. This shows use of the noble blade, or "trashy cultivation," on the vineyard. All the weeds would be killed by a large blade, cutting six inches underneath the ground, and then left to lie on the ground for protection from the wind. *Cal Poly Special Collections.*

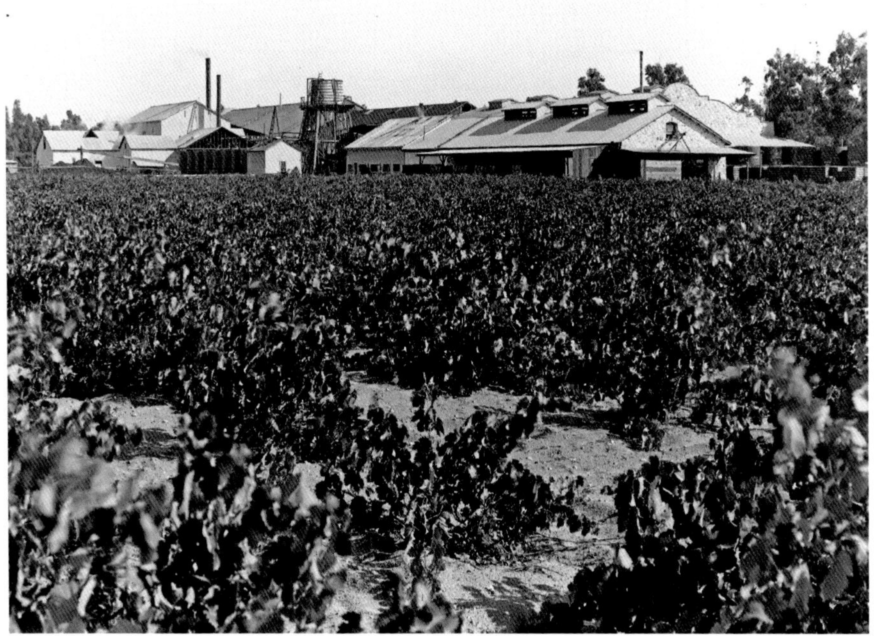

Three cellars and the boiler room at the back end of the winery. Cellar number one is on the left, then cellar number two and finally cellar number three with the cupolas on top. Cellar number four is underneath cellar number three. The vines are four to five years old. *Cal Poly Special Collections.*

Guasti's unwavering faith in his dream paid off. In the fifth year after the vines had been planted, a winter storm coming down from the mountains laid bare a strip of land where some of the vines had been planted. Something miraculous had happened: their roots had descended into the ground twenty-five feet. This had been made possible because of the loam that existed there, and the roots had found their way to the moist soil deep beneath the desert sand above, which enabled them to survive scorching sun and drought.

Additional acreage was purchased, including Antonio Signorio's original 640 acres, which became known as Ranch II. Also, 84 acres were set aside, and in 1904, construction began on the first building units in the Guasti. The land was contained by Archibald Avenue on the east, the Southern Railroad depot on the south, Turner Avenue to the north and Route 66 to the west. These were rock structures, constructed of stone brought from Ranch II to the north. Three mission-style winery buildings were built; the largest was 100 by 200 feet. A fermenting cellar was constructed and measured 54 by 450 feet, which at the time was the largest one in the world.

Many of the settlements and farms in the rockier areas had to remove stones from their property, and they were used to construct homes, barns and other buildings they needed. "The biggest venture in the use of stone in buildings was done by Guasti. He had land holdings up in the upper end of the valley against the mountains known as Ranch Number Two," explained Philo Biane in an interview in 1992. "In clearing that area, he accumulated a lot of stones. They were hauled by wagon and mules about seven miles down to the Guasti location which was more or less in the center of the valley. The rocks were constructed into the winery, the cooper shop, the distillery and the fermenting room. All of them were built of stone."

The original holding tanks within the new winery could hold twenty-five thousand and forty-five thousand gallons of wine, respectively. They also built a building to make spirits and fortify wine that measured forty-two by seventy-nine feet. It included a steel and wood cooperage (making barrels), a still tower, concrete storage tanks, a distillery, a boiler room, a refrigeration

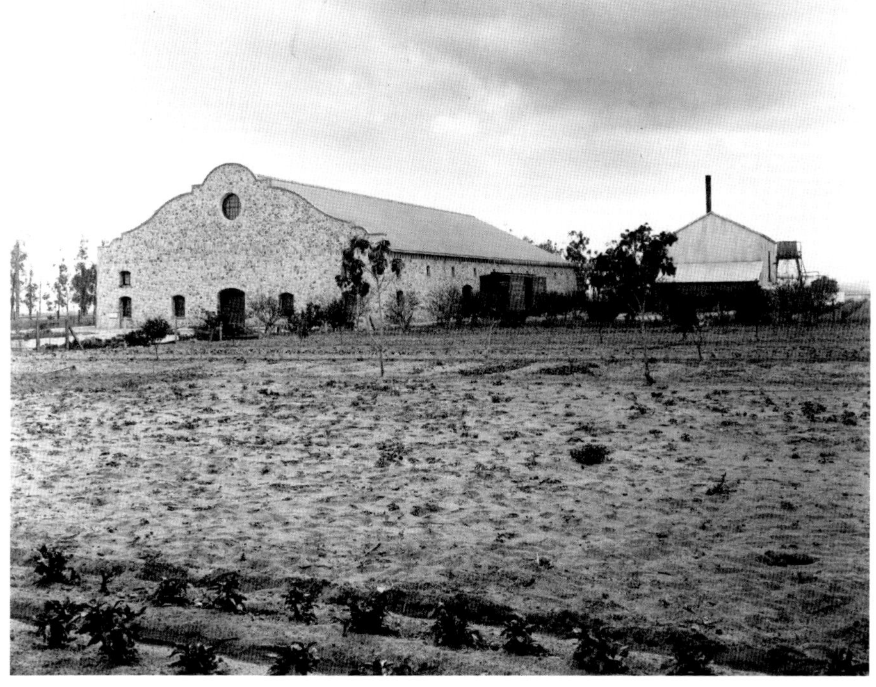

Early picture (1906–7) of cellar number one and part of the room at the east end of the winery. A railroad car is on the track toward the center. *Cal Poly Special Collections.*

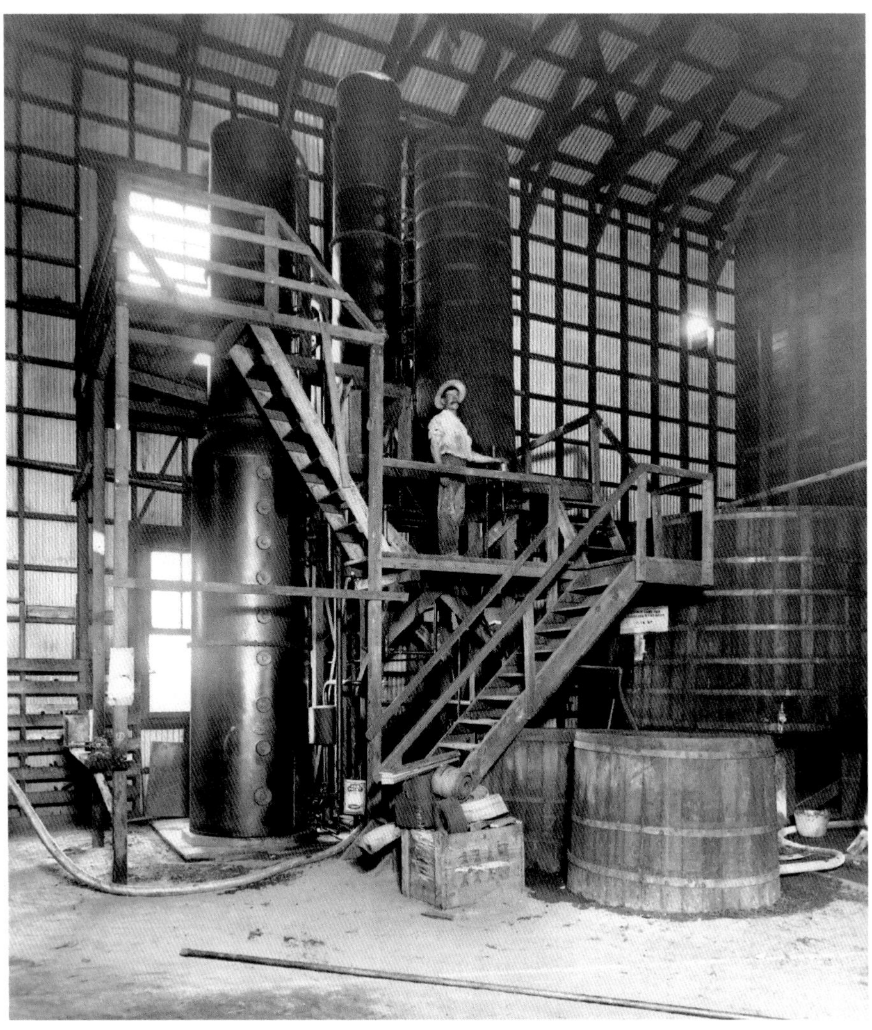

Distillery operator standing on the framework of an early version of a continuous pot still built by Mr. Levy of Los Angeles. Each one of the little openings is really a little still in and of itself. The wine enters the top of the still and goes through the still with an ever-increasing alcohol content. The operator kept checking the alcohol level of the dispatch by putting his finger in the material and tasting it. *Cal Poly Special Collections.*

room, an aging room, a compressor room and a concentrating room. The building served as a power plant for the rest of the winery buildings.

"The main building was six hundred feet long," Philo Biane recalled. "It was built in three sections, cellar number one, cellar number two and cellar number three. Each of the three sections were three foot at the base and two foot at the top. The walls were twenty-three feet high. The ceiling was made of steel galvanized iron: fabricated steel rafters, sheeted with sheet metal."

The boilers fed the still, an ammonia machine was used for the refrigeration and there were pumps to send water to the cooling towers. The men in the cooper shop were able to produce two hundred oak or redwood barrels per day. The barrels produced were not only used on the premises but were also sold to other local wineries. The iron used to band the barrels and other items used at the winery was created at the blacksmith shop on site.

"When we came to California we found no oak that was usable for creating tanks, or even barrels," Philo Biane recalled.

> *We did find California Redwood, a good wood to use to make quite large tanks. These tanks varied from five hundred gallons up to one hundred*

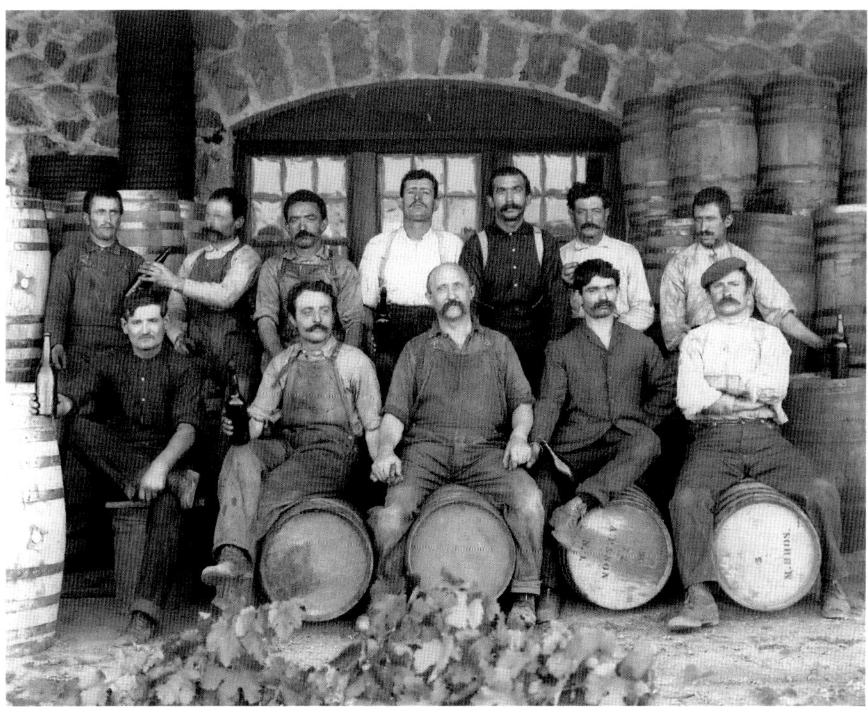

The cooper shop workers at the Italian Vineyard Company in front of the winery's shop. This cooper shop was run by Mr. Danzo, who is seated in the center of the picture here. The men standing in the rear are Italians whom Mr. Guasti invited to come over to the United States and work in the winery. Note that each man is holding his own bottle of wine. Each winery worker was provided his own bottle of wine for lunch and another bottle to enjoy with dinner. This benefit did not extend to the migrants working in the vineyards. *Cal Poly Special Collection.*

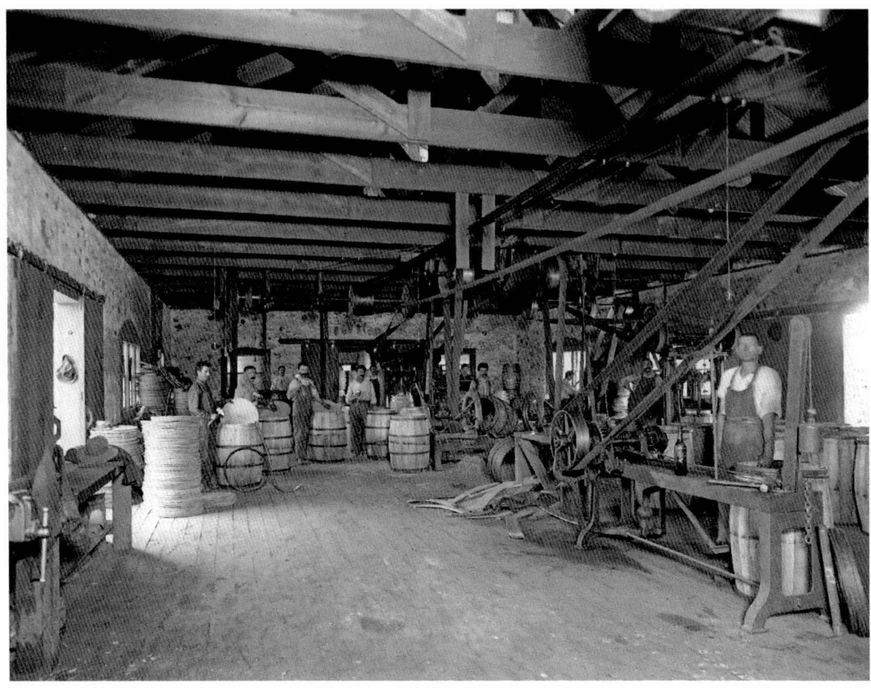

Interior view of the cooper shop showing several workers, tools and heavy machines used in making barrels. On the left is a workman ready to put on the barrel head. Next, he would put on the hoops and then machine-drive the hoops onto the barrel. Another man is seen working on a croze machine, which cuts the grooves in the staves to make a barrel. One of these original machines still exists today at the Mountain Vista Winery in Rancho Cucamonga. *Cal Poly Special Collections.*

> *thousand gallons. They were held together with steel bands. The California Redwood grew so straight that it could produce a good three-inch stave in thickness, and be as high as twenty feet.*
>
> *After World War II, the use of cement in building a tank came into being. We patterned these tanks after the work that was done by the French in Algiers. They used cement because there was no good wood available there. The tanks made with cement were fairly good for holding wine. Most of the capacities were in the fifty- to sixty-thousand-gallon range. You could build them in a series and use a common wall for two or more tanks. That became very prevalent in the cooperage area of the wine industry. The next step was going into the stainless-steel tanks after World War II.*

Guasti wanted the best for his winery and would seek out the best experts and workers. When he needed a grafter for his vines in 1906, he found

Antonio Martinez, a respected horticulturist from Salamanca, Spain, and brought him to work for him at the winery.

Guasti ran winery operations from his office on Palmetto Street in Los Angeles. The two-story ranch house was used by the Italian Vineyard Company stockholders for its meetings. The Guasti family used the house when they visited the vineyards. The house, called the "Big House," did not have the opulence of the family's home in Los Angeles, but it was large and comfortable during their visits. The first child born in Guasti was Signorio's son, Alfred, and in 1903, he was christened in the Big House; Mrs. Guasti was his godmother.

In 1910, the town was officially named Guasti following a post office name change on October 16, 1910. The first post office at this location, established on March 22, 1887, was originally known as Zucker, named after the original postmaster, Fred Zucker. A railroad depot called South Cucamonga contained the original post office. The town of Guasti grew quickly to three hundred people comprising about fifty families who settled in the area, all of whom were interested in working the vineyards Guasti helped build. A school was built for the children, and the community began to grow into a real township.

By 1917, the Cucamonga-Guasti vineyard spanned more than twenty thousand acres and was heralded as the world's largest contiguous vineyard. They transformed a literal desert into a prosperous vineyard, with vines that stretched for as far as the eye could see in every direction.

EXPANSION

In 1918, Guasti again became very ill. This time it was during an epidemic of influenza that plagued the area. He recovered, and the vineyard continued to flourish into Prohibition. In 1920, Guasti built a reading room at the vineyard for the benefit of the employees in Guasti with the assistance of the county librarian.

In 1923, plans were made for the construction of a $75,000 mansion on the site of the old Guasti ranch home. The architects chosen for the project were Morgan, Walls and Morgan of Los Angeles. Groundbreaking on the house was held on April 19, 1923, and the construction was done by Campbell Construction, out of Ontario. It was built in the Italian Renaissance Revival style. Included in the house plans were an aviary, spacious gardens, a swimming pool and tennis courts. The house was completed in 1924 and was known as the La Villa Guasti. In a California guidebook, it was referred to as the finest private estate in San Bernardino County.

Other developments included the introduction of a hog and dairy farm. It was an effort to diversify the agricultural interests of Guasti, but it also used the manure as a fertilizer for the vineyards. Guasti had four hundred Berkshire hogs, which were known for being ideal for breeding.

The dairy farm had thirty-five registered Guernsey cows, and like his winery, the dairy was known for its high standard of sanitation processes. The purpose was to breed cows for other local farms, and the milk was sold to customers in Los Angeles. The cows bred at the dairy won awards at the 1922 California State Fair.

Guasti was very keen about the sanitation and cleanliness of the facilities, and they became the model for other wineries that came after. Every two weeks, the entire facility was completely washed top to bottom. The wine produced by Guasti quickly gained notoriety and began winning

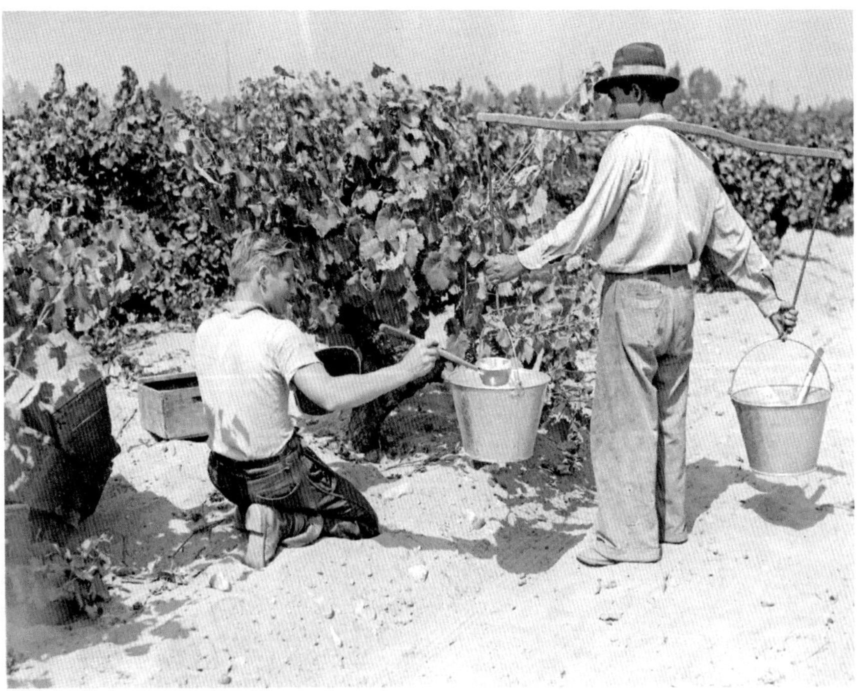

Nothing is overlooked in the way of comfort for the field workers in the Guasti Vineyards, and here, one of the water men serves a harvest worker with a cooling drink. The arid, sandy land is ideal for grape growing. *Cal Poly Special Collections.*

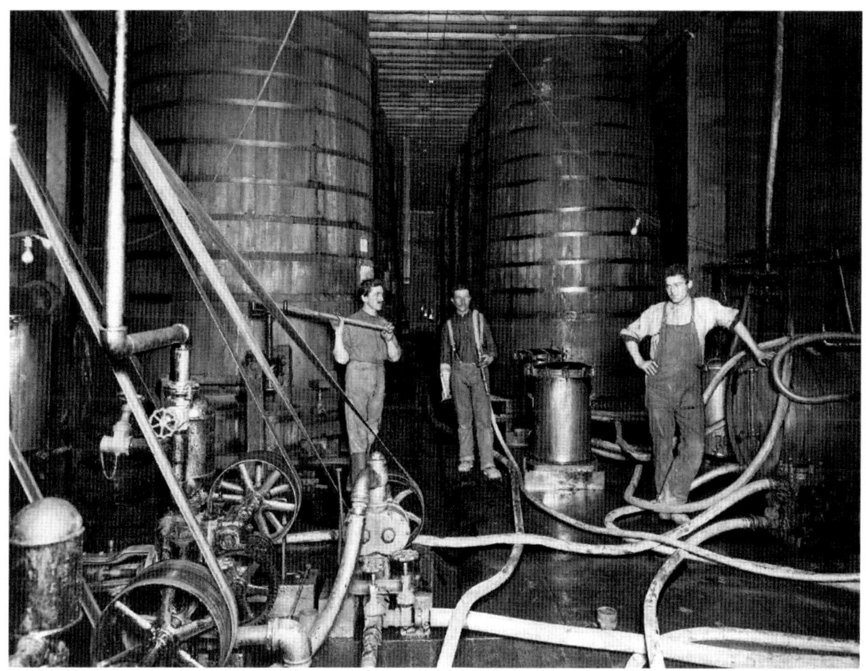

Interior scene of cellar number one, showing pumps that are driven by a line shaft, as well as many hoses for conveying the wine. To the lower right are wine filter screens. The men are seen replacing the screens after having cleaned them of debris. *Cal Poly Special Collections.*

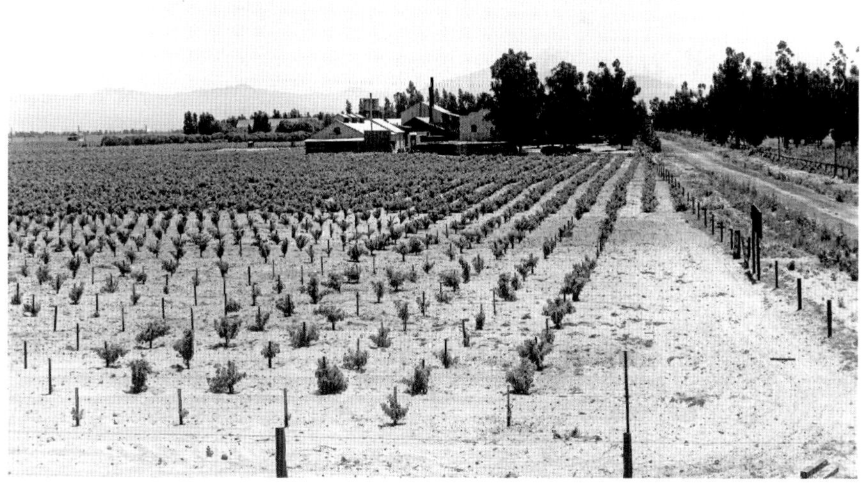

The back end of the winery, looking north, showing the buildings constructed for the raisin industry during World War I, as well as a section of the stone fermenting room. *Cal Poly Special Collections.*

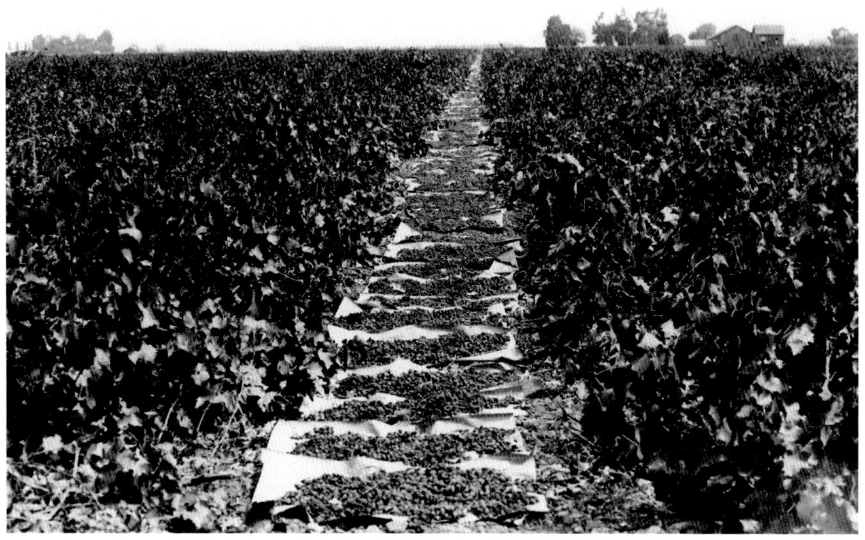

Vineyards adapted to growing raisin grapes for the World War I food growing effort. The grapes were laid on paper trays to be dried. Later, a dehydrator was built to dry the grapes without the fear of rain spoiling the crop. *Cal Poly Special Collections.*

gold and silver medals at competitions around the world and at exhibitions such as the Trans-Mississippi Exposition and the Exposition Universelle at Paris. The vineyard produced port, sherry, Angelica, Muscatel, Zinfandel, Claret, Burgundy, Burga, Riesling, Sauterne and more. As it grew, it began to develop branch houses in New York, New Orleans and Chicago.

EXPERIMENTAL VINEYARDS

Guasti's original vineyard success had attracted the attention of the Department of Agriculture. He had turned a desert into a huge agricultural wonder. With the help of Guasti, a patch of the land was used for further experimentation with other varieties of vines to determine which vines were the best adapted to growing in the region. They planted 492 different varieties of grapes, and many of the grapes still used in California are from the varieties that had been grown there.

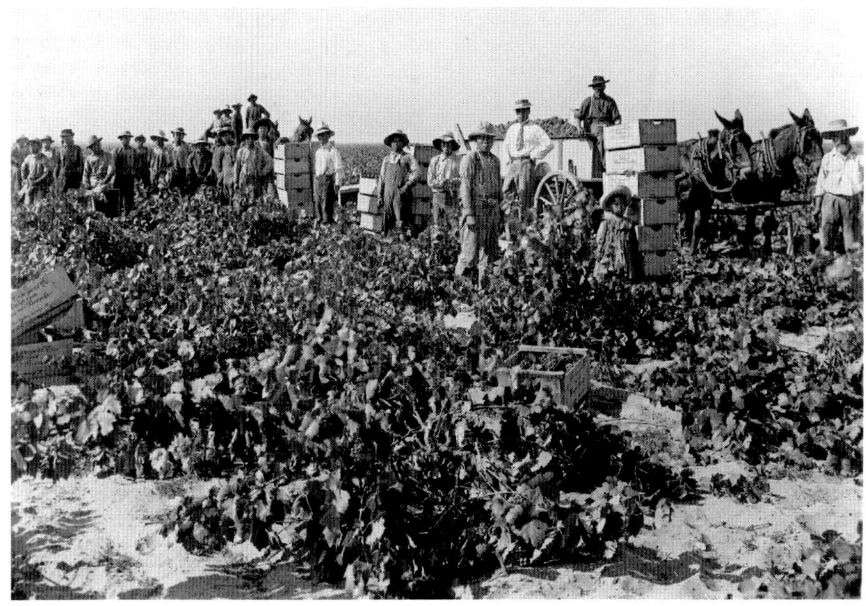

Early photo of field workers hauling out grapes with mule wagons before the arrival of the railroad. The workers look mostly Mexican, but there may be some African Americans. The boxes are labeled "Italian Vineyard Co." *Cal Poly Special Collections.*

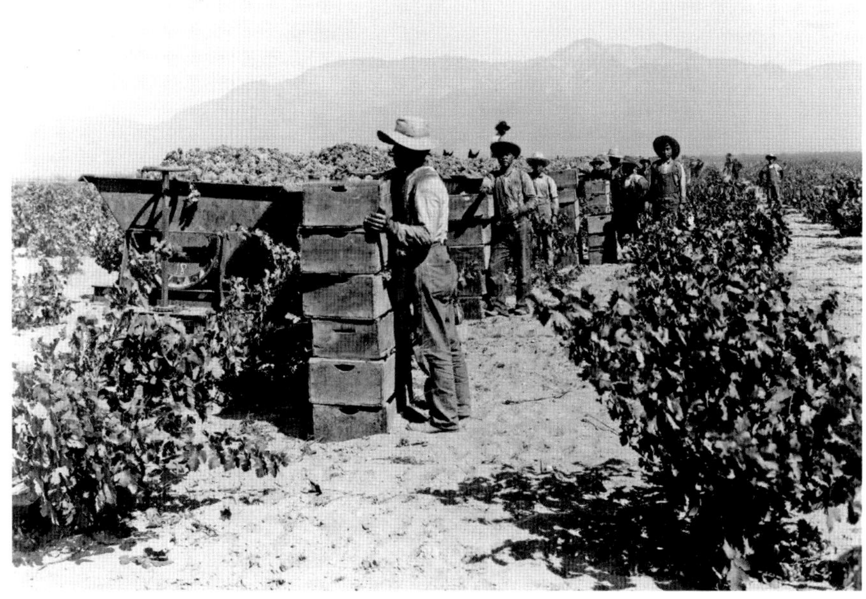

Grape pickers and harvest workers bringing grapes to the temporary railroad line. Due to the extensiveness of the vineyards and the sandy soil, a temporary line with little gondola cars was used to bring the harvest into the winery. *Cal Poly Special Collections.*

RAIL LINE

Guasti had a miniature railroad line with a custom-made steam locomotive built for the workers that reached out into the vineyard, carrying tons of grapes picked by the workers to huge troughs, where the grapes were dumped. The train, with its forty cars, replaced the mules they had been using. The rail line ran twenty-two miles along the side of the vineyards.

Guasti was very proud of his winery and the fact that he had the most modern and mechanized winery at that time. During the harvest season, the grapes were handpicked and sent to winery using the gondola cars by way of his personal railroad. The grapes were sent by conveyor to a large concrete basin, where they were crushed.

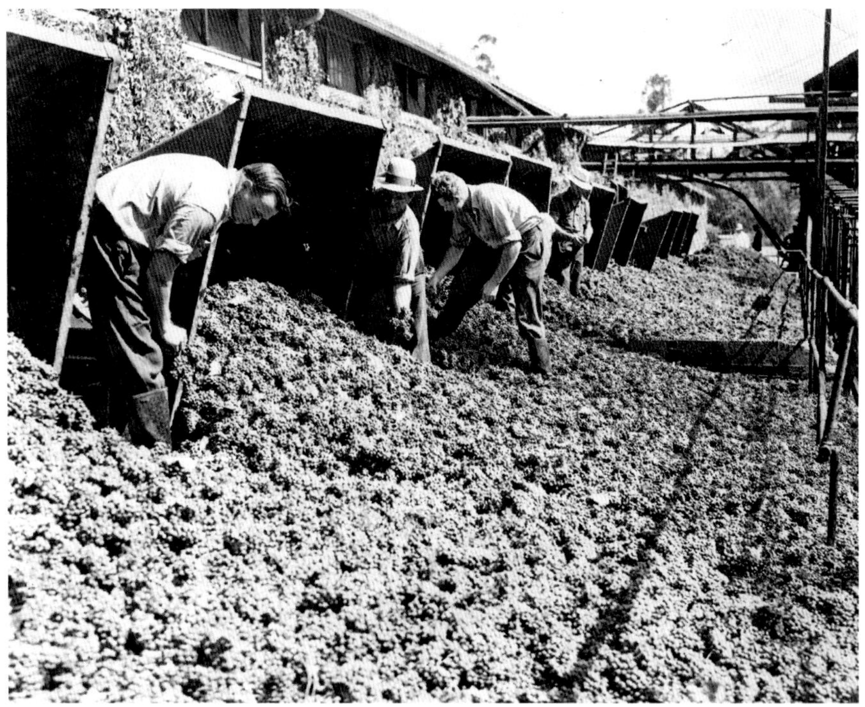

Workmen are unloading the gondola cars on which part of California's record grape crop is brought in from the vineyards to the winery at Guasti. The greatest bulk of the record crop was estimated at 2.6 million tons (equaling 5 billion, 220 million pounds). *Cal Poly Special Collections.*

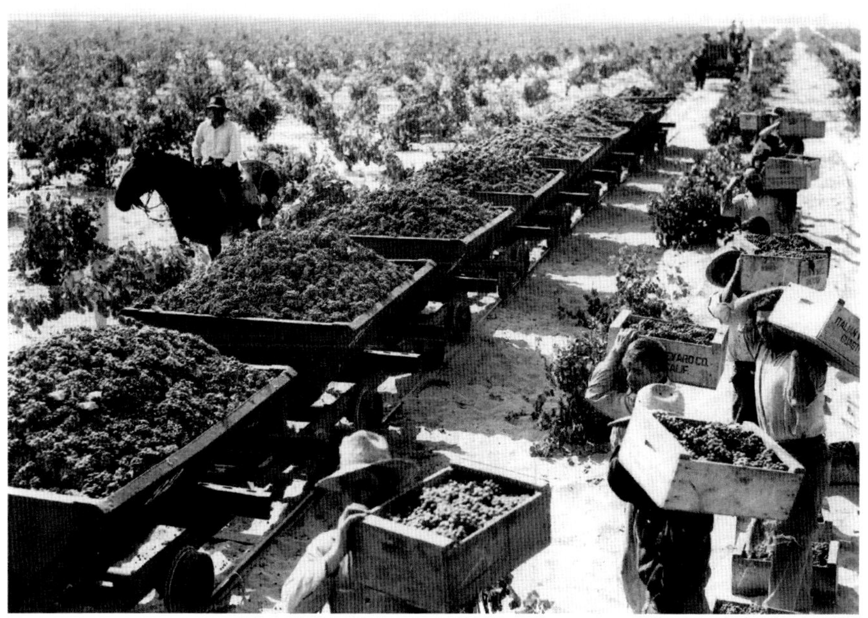

A busy scene in one of the world's largest vineyards at Guasti, California. Workers are loading the wine product on a train, which gathers in the product from six thousand acres of vines. *Associated Press photo, October 18, 1933.*

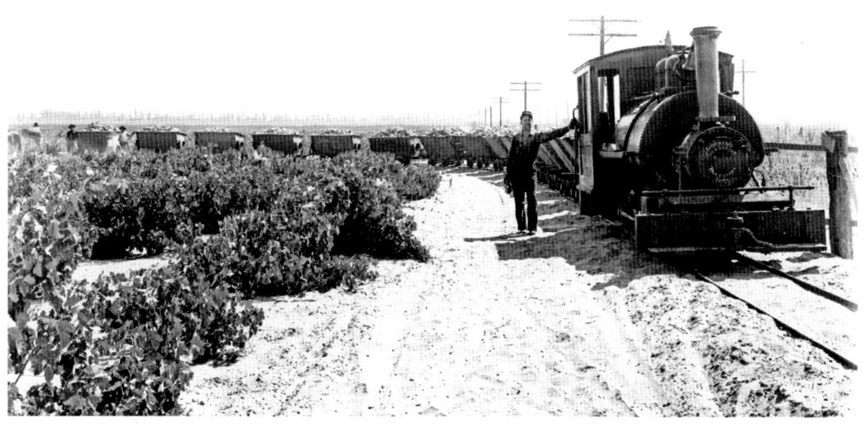

The small engine and gondola cars head back to the winery on the temporary track laid in the vineyards. *Cal Poly Special Collections.*

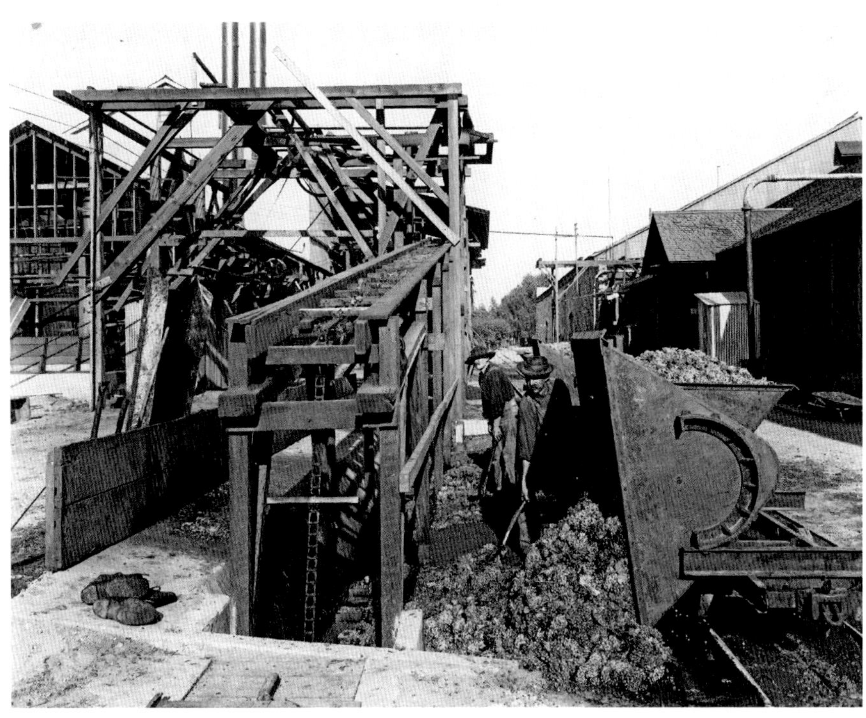

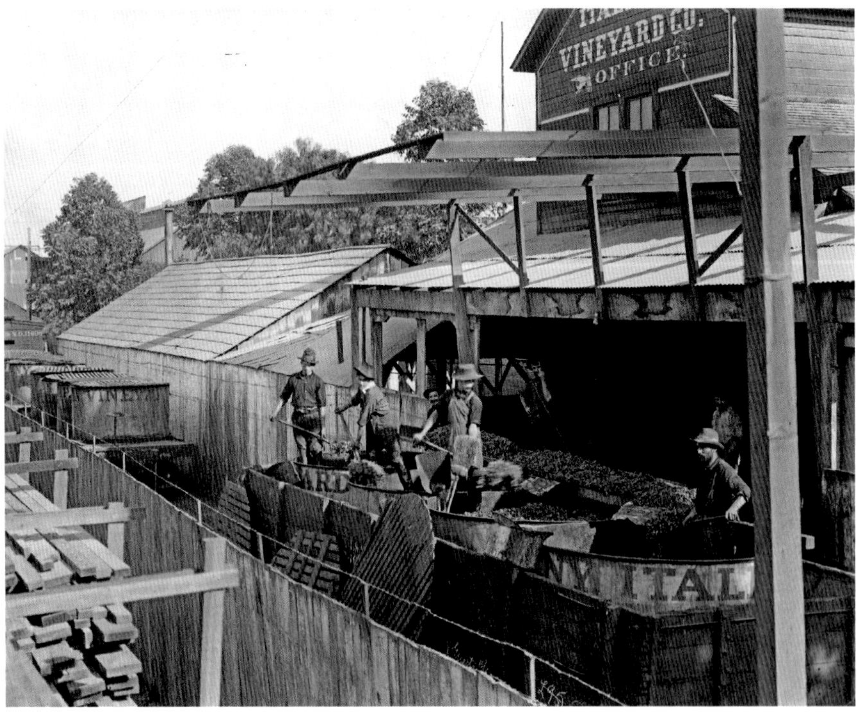
VINEYARD CO.
OFFICE.

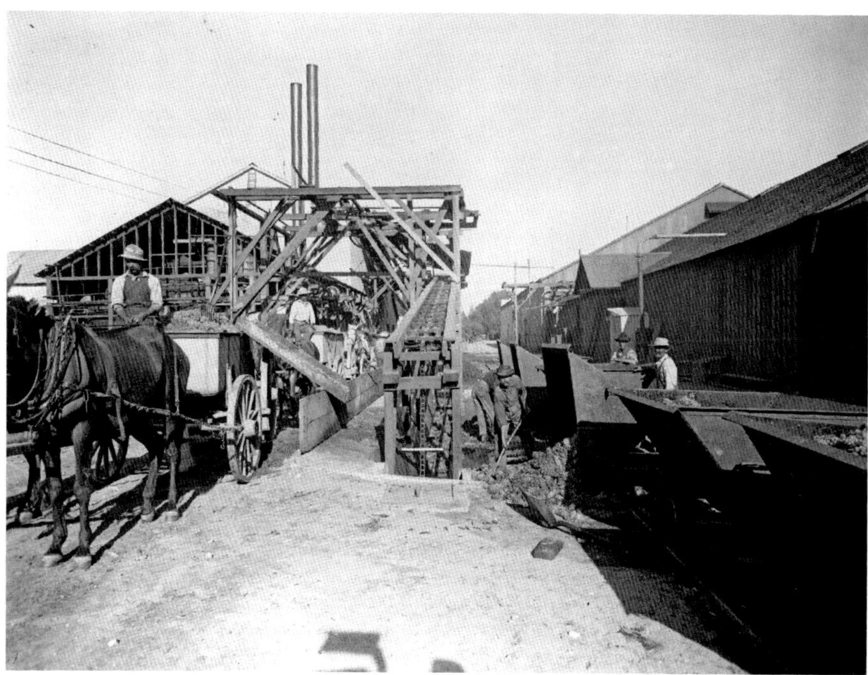

Above: A view of the boiler room. The workmen are shoveling grapes onto the conveyor to be conveyed into the crusher and then pumped to the fermenting tanks. *Cal Poly Special Collections.*

Opposite, top: Workers shoveling grapes from the gondola cars, with the train tracks, crusher and Fermenting Room visible. The gondola wouldn't empty completely, so the remaining grapes needed to be hand shoveled onto the conveyor. The conveyor would take the grapes to the crusher, and then from the crusher they would finally be pumped to the Fermenting Room tanks. *Cal Poly Special Collections.*

Opposite, bottom: Men shoveling grapes recently harvested from the fields onto a conveyor. The railroad car that would be used to bring grapes to the winery had four tanks, as vineyards could be quite a distance from the winery. The weight of the grapes caused juice to come out, so slats were placed in the bottom of the table for the juice to run out through a valve for collection. *Cal Poly Special Collections.*

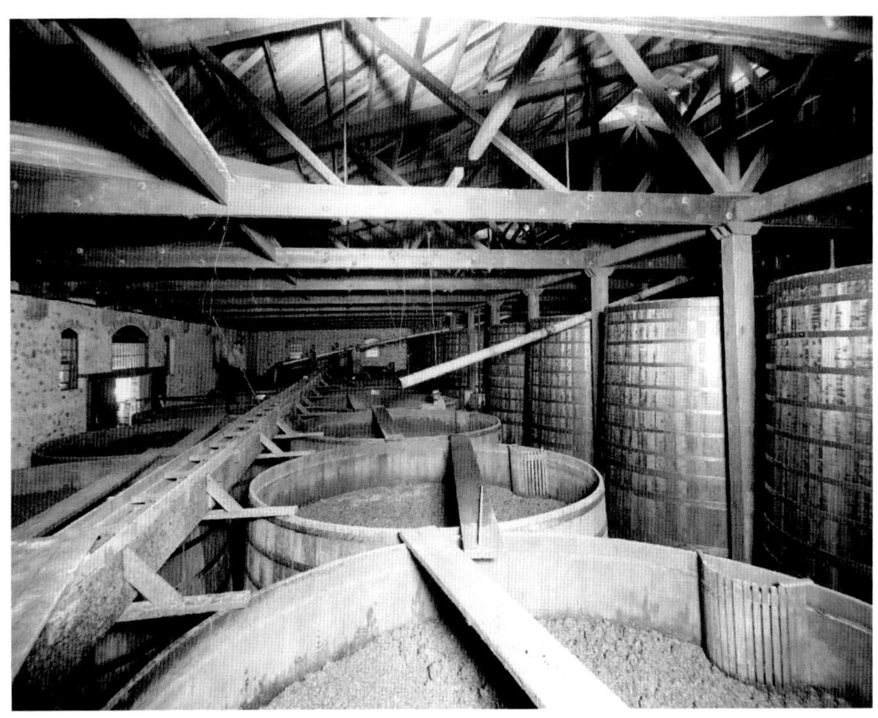

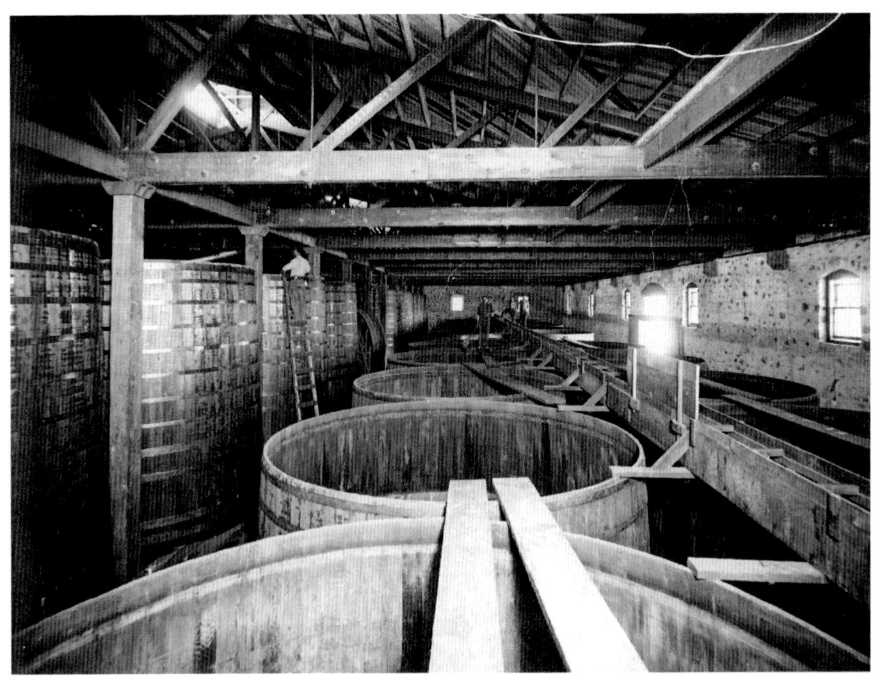

The grape juice, or must, was pumped into the open fermentation tanks. The juice was inoculated with cultured wine yeast, and sulfur was added to kill bacteria and wild yeasts. The workers would risk their lives walking on planks between the vats to check on the fermenting liquid. This could be dangerous because high amounts of carbon dioxide would build in the rafters, and this could cause a worker to pass out into one of the vats.

After the fermentation process was completed, the liquid went through a filtering process during which seeds, skins and other debris were separated from the wine. The wine would undergo a pasteurization and cooling process, and then it was aged.

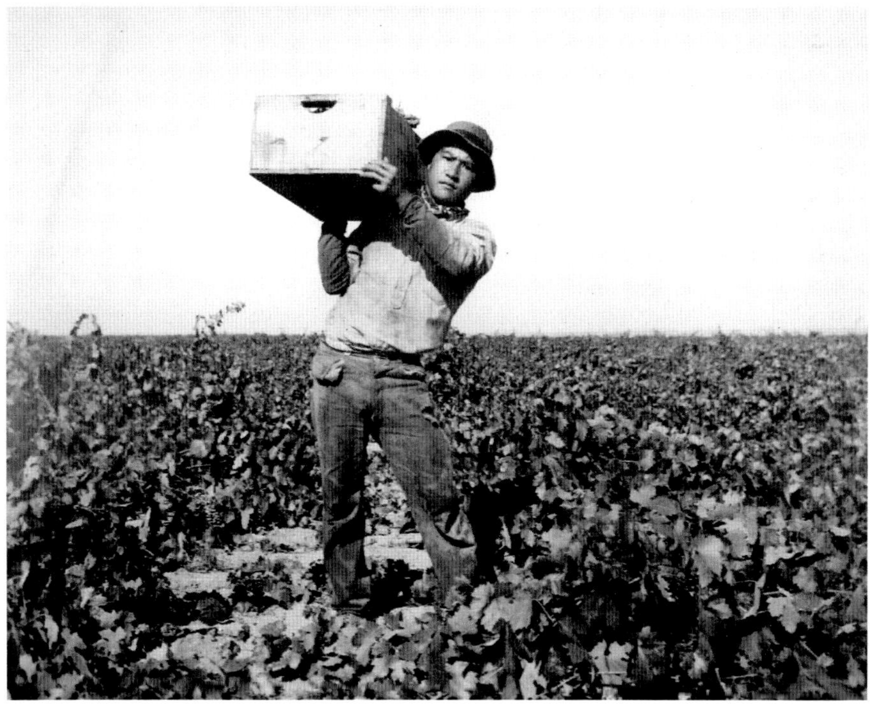

Above: Workers harvesting grapes in the field by hand. Each year, twenty to twenty-five thousand tons (40 to 45 million pounds) of grapes were brought into the winery. Grape harvest workers were usually Mexican migrants and had their own camp near the vineyards. *Cal Poly Special Collections.*

Opposite, top: Six-thousand-gallon tanks inside the Fermenting Room. Two small train tracks running between the crushers are visible. *Cal Poly Special Collections.*

Opposite, bottom: Interior of fermenting tanks and conveyor belt in view. Also, large boards are seen lying on top of the empty tanks for walkways for the workers, who walked along the top of the fermenters as they checked the temperature and the balling or sugar content of the juice every two hours. *Cal Poly Special Collections.*

MEXICAN CAMP

In 1926, plans were made for the construction of an up-to-date camp for the employees at Guasti. This was a number of years before the introduction of the Bracero Program, but there were a lot of Mexican laborers who lived there, which is why they referred to it as the "Mexican Camp." It was located south of the railroad tracks and to the west of Turner Avenue. The cost for camp was $50,000, and each unit had electricity.

Many of the year-round workers were from Italy, France and Spain because they were some of the best and most experienced workers. Guasti provided these workers shared quarters, and for those who had families, it provided them cottages. A clubhouse with two dormitories, showers and bathtubs was provided for the single men. There were still shortages in the number of laborers needed during picking season. There were quite a few Japanese workers used as pickers as well, around three hundred. Even though there was a level of distrust from employers of Japanese people during this time in history, they had little choice, as it was hard to find workers willing to work on a temporary basis in the extremely hot conditions.

There were also some Chinese laborers who had worked off their contracted service with the Pacific Railroad. The contracts usually lasted ten years, and they were granted the ability to live in the United States. But they needed a way to make a living, so they were also used as regular and temporary laborers. Even after the picking season, there was the large task of pruning the vines in December. Smoke hung in the air for weeks as the prunings were burned. Guasti insisted on a clean, orderly vineyard. There was also a large stable of one hundred head of stock that were kept in order be used on the grounds.

Each ethnic group developed its own camp—Mexican, Asian and African American—in a self-segregated fashion. At the height of the vineyard, about 1,200 lived in these laborer camps.

The year 1926 was also the first when Easter morning services were held in the new Catholic church built in Guasti. The church was not quite complete at the time of the service. Construction continued until later that year and cost about $40,000. The project was started in 1924 by Guasti and his wife. They wanted to build a church as a replica of the seventeenth-century church in Asti, near where Secondo was born. Guasti brought stonemasons and woodworkers from Mexico to complete the church.

The courtyard was lined with stone walls and filled with a garden and white statues of saints. Inside the sanctuary were bare wooden beams with wrought-iron chandeliers. The walls depicted biblical scenes, and the stained-glass window depicted St. Secundus, who was beheaded in Asti during Hadrian the Conqueror's rule.

When the colony was first established, school for the children in primary grades was taught in the Big House. As the colony grew, a larger space was needed, so Guasti built a brick schoolhouse on Turner Avenue for the children. It was called the Piedmont School in honor of the region in Northern Italy where Guasti was raised. The building was deeded to the Piedmont School District for five dollars with the understanding that if the property were ever used for anything but a school for twelve months, the title would revert to the Italian Vineyard Company. Once the children graduated from the primary grades, they had to go to the high school in Ontario, which was four miles away. In 1935, the Piedmont School was destroyed by a fire. In 1939, it was rebuilt with architect H.L. Gogery and engineer R.S. Barnes. It was named the Louisa M. Guasti School.

Guasti and his wife had four children, and his son Secondo Guasti Jr. was born on April 14, 1891. Secondo Jr. helped his father manage the Italian Vineyard Company. While Guasti attended to the winery, Louisa became the matriarch of the colony that had been built there. She took an interest in the children and adults in the community and attended to their comfort and happiness.

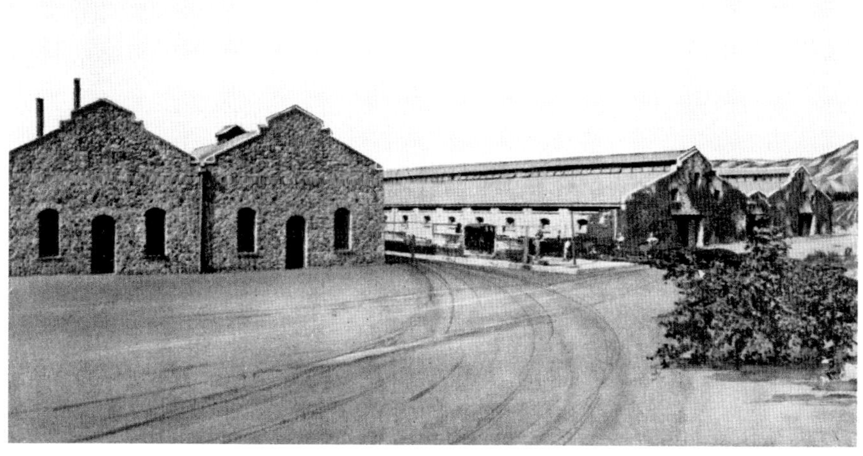

Spirit and Fortification Rooms of the Italian Vineyard Company's Plant. The fermenting cellars could hold 1 million gallons of wine. *Cal Poly Special Collections.*

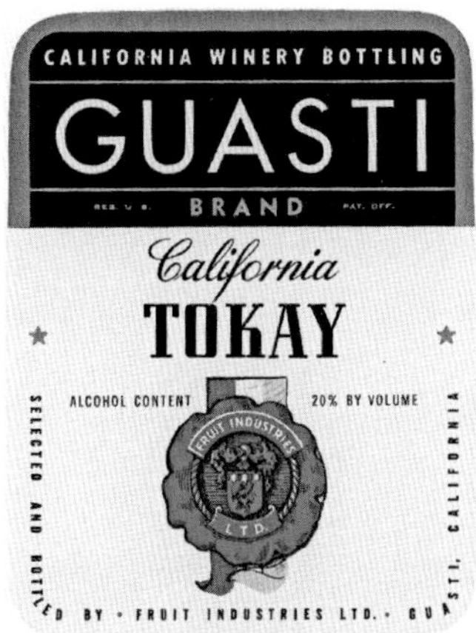

Guasti was one of the original wine producers in the Cucamonga region. *Cal Poly Special Collections.*

Mrs. Guasti organized activities for the children. She would have parties and barbecues often at the ranch. Around Easter, there would be grand egg hunts, and for Christmas, there was always a large decorated tree for everyone to enjoy. They even celebrated Vento di Settembre (A Harvest Celebration) as it was celebrated back in Italy.

Prior to Prohibition, Guasti was appointed by the governor as a member of the State Board of Viticultural Commissioners, which was a newly created body designed to conduct a campaign of education throughout the state for the improvement of their $150 million viticultural industry.

In 1913, the grape growers and winemakers in Southern California met in Cucamonga to form the Southern California Grape Protective Association. The purpose was to educate people and oppose the Eighteenth Amendment and Prohibition. Guasti was elected president of the association.

On August 28, 1927, at the age of sixty-seven, Secondo Guasti died in his home in Los Angeles. His son took over as president of the Italian Vineyard Company. The Guasti estate was valued at $1.2 million at the time of Guasti's death. He was opposed to Prohibition and never believed that it would last. Just before his death, he ordered that a large walnut grove be torn down and planted with more grapes.

At the start of Prohibition, the winery had to make some changes to the products it offered because it could no longer produce wine for sale. So, it began to create medicinal wines. These wines contained pepsin, beef extract and iron and were supposed to be health tonics. It also began producing sacramental wines on the Padre label. Like many other wineries, it began to ship tons of grapes east to home winemakers. Every day, the men made boxes for the Zinfandel grapes to put on the boxcars.

Zinfandel grapes were a stable grape for shipping. They had a balling of 24 (sugar content) which made a 12 percent alcohol wine, which was great for home winemakers. The problem with some of the homemade wines is that they would turn bad by April, so the vineyard tried to create as high an alcohol content wine as possible in order for it to last until the following summer. The boxcars had sulfur pots smoking on them to prevent the grapes from turning bad before they arrived at their destinations in the East.

"Prohibition created a new industry for us which was the shipping of grapes," said Philo Biane.

> *This change also affected all the things that led up to the picking of the grapes. For example, the fruit had to have a much sounder nature as it had to be able to stand up to shipment from here to New York in a fresh state. At that time, all we had was the "iced reefers," we didn't have any mechanical refrigeration on the trains. That also led to the making of lug boxes, which was a good employment for young men at that time. There was also the lidding of grapes in the field, and then loading the grapes in the car and nailing them with long strips in position so they could make the trip to the eastern coast. It actually set up as an occupation for certain of us that were involved in the grape industry.*

In addition, the winery was given special permission to produce eight thousand gallons of jelly created from wine each year. Under the agreement, one thousand gallons of wine at a time were transferred from the winery to a special government-bonded warehouse. The wine was then kept under lock and key and protected by a sheriff's deputy.

Prohibition continued. In 1929, a decision was made to change the company, and Fruit Industries Ltd. was created. The purpose was to find new ways to market grapes and grape products. "We had another economic problem in the United States and we went into a very serious depression," Philo Bianc recalled. "At that point, the people on the eastern seaboard could not afford to buy our grapes and we lost that market. Because of the Depression and the very sad state the grape grower was in, the operators of the various vineyards throughout the whole state decided to band together and work out something that could create another market. The Fruit Industries was created under those conditions."

The Italian Vineyard Company, Garrett & Company and Cucamonga Growers were a part of the merger of the Fruit Industries Ltd. Other organizations involved were California Grape Product Company, National Fruit Products, Colonial Grape Products, the California Wine Association, Community Grape Corporation and Earl Fruit. At the time of the merger, the Italian Vineyard Company had increased to five thousand acres of vineyard.

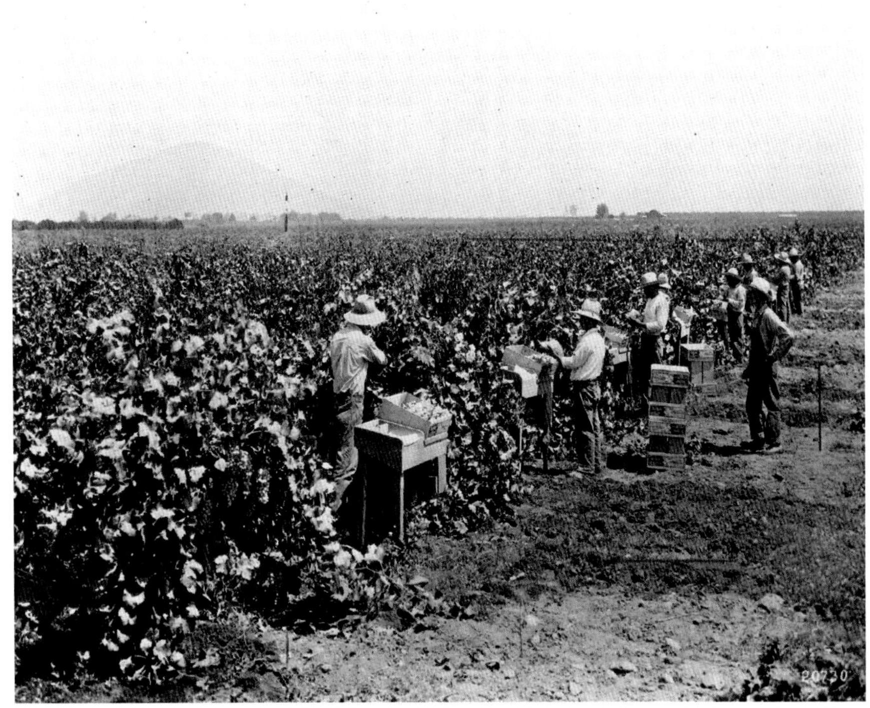
20730

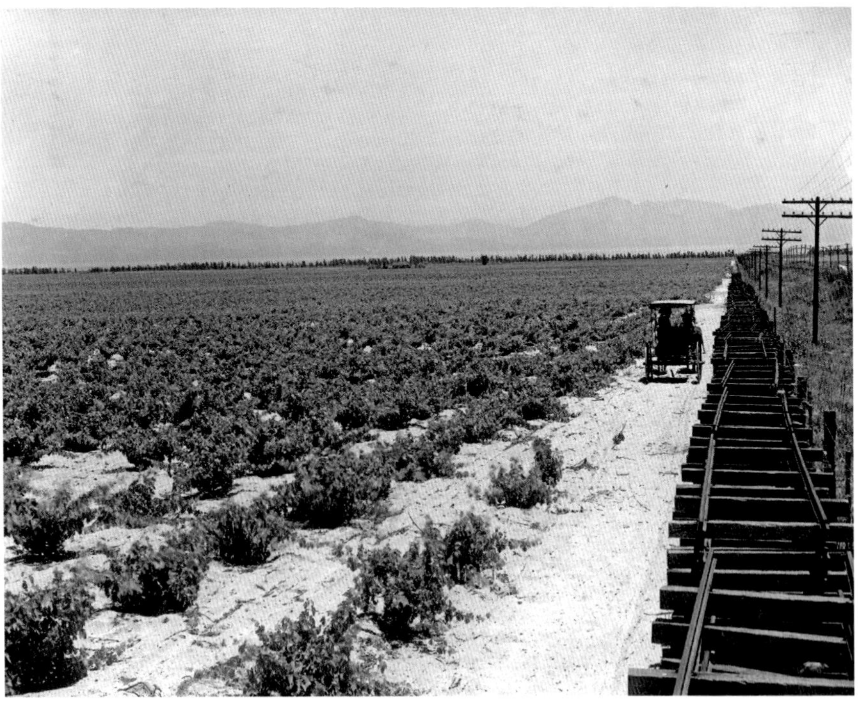

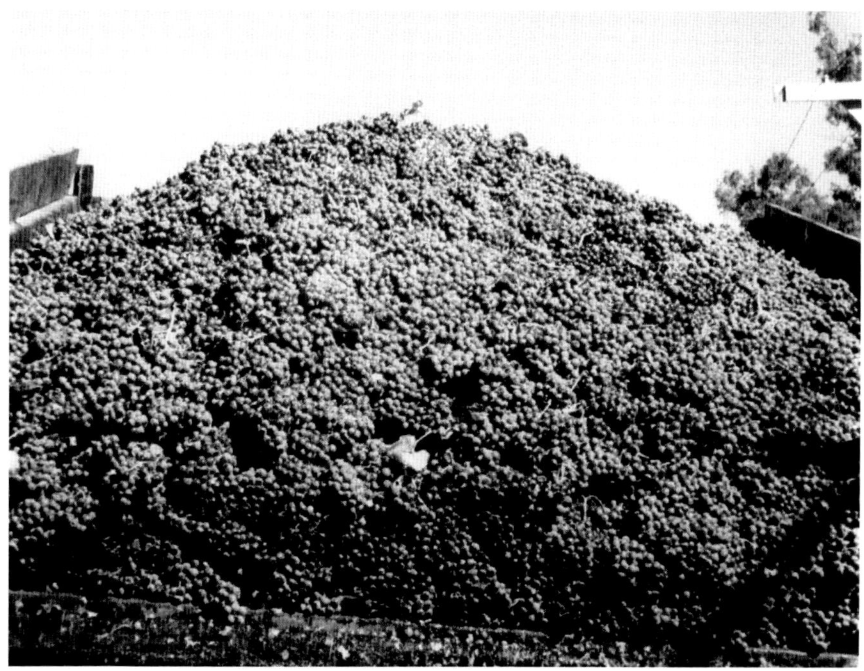

Above: Grape harvest in 1936, Guasti, California. *Cal Poly Special Collections.*

Opposite, top: At the Guasti Vineyards, workers gently wrap grape bunches and place them in boxes ready for shipment to home winemakers across the nation. *Cal Poly Special Collections.*

Opposite, bottom: A young vineyard, with the temporary narrow-gauge railroad track on the sandy soil used to transport the grapes to the winery. It was very heavy work. Each section of the track needed four men to lay it down and bolt it together. *Cal Poly Special Collections.*

Fruit Industries represented more than 80 percent of the vineyards in the Cucamonga Valley, and because of this, it was able to get federal assistance in the form of a loan of $20 million from Commodity Credit, a government program. This enabled the group to establish plants in Guasti that could concentrate grape juice into syrup. This syrup could be used in different industries, such as the baking industry, as a substitute for sugar. The concentrate could also be shipped to home winemakers to use to make wine—the product was known as Vine-Glo.

In the 1930s, the Italian Vineyard Company had grown to become the largest employer and industrial organization in western San Bernardino County. It was valued at $3 million and employed more than one thousand laborers during the harvest seasons, with a payroll of $282,000 per year.

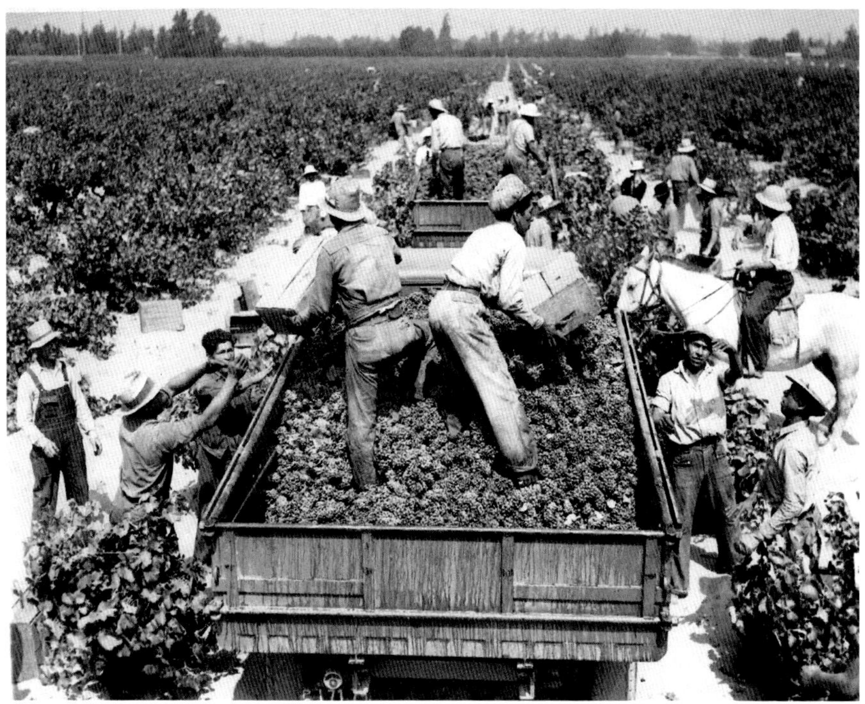

It's harvest time in the Guasti fields, and the company trucks make the rounds, collecting the grapes for transportation to the winery and the crushers. Only 25 percent of the winery workers were Italian immigrants, while the others are Americans. In the fields, the greater percentage of workers are Mexicans migrants. The regular workers live in permanent houses, while the seasonal workers (migrants) live in tents. Photo taken on October 26, 1937. *Cal Poly Special Collections.*

They picked twenty thousand tons of grapes, which were then processed into 5 million gallons of wine.

Trucks replaced the rail line, and a new bottling, shipping and storage plant was built, as well as a new warehouses and garages for the trucks and vehicles. A sewage system was established in the colony that drained into the middle of town and then to a reservoir.

In 1933, Secondo Guasti Jr. died of uremia. He was only forty-two years old. J.A. Barlotti took over the operation and became the president of the Italian Vineyard Company and of Fruit Industries. That same year, Prohibition was repealed, and the Italian Vineyard Company pulled out of Fruit Industries and became independent once again.

In 1941, the Italian Vineyard Company built a building at the cost of $50,000 to house champagne. It also spent another $51,000

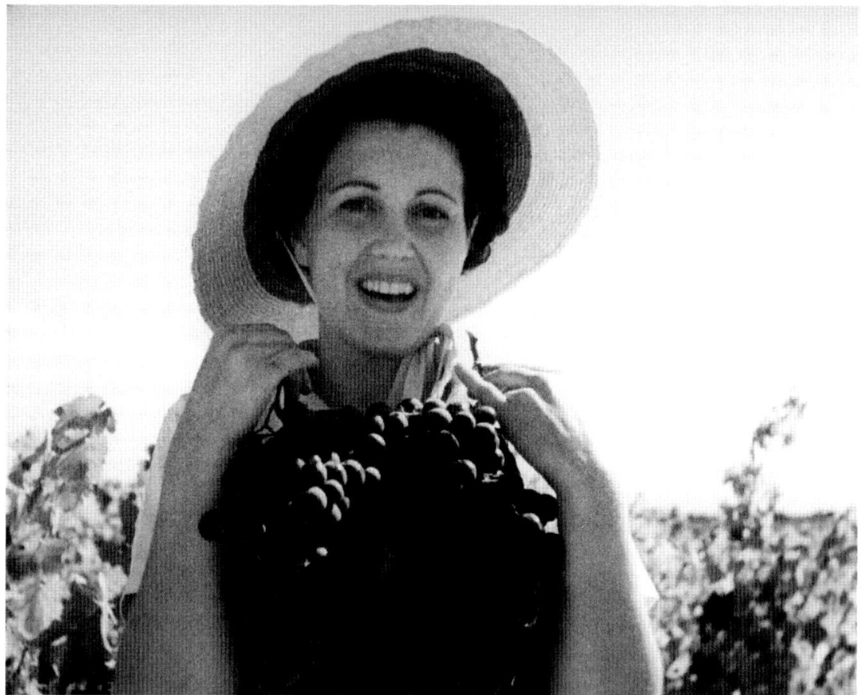

Guasti grape harvest, October 13, 1937. *Cal Poly Special Collections.*

expanding other buildings and facilities at the winery. This increased the winery's storage capacity from 2 million gallons to 3.5 million gallons. The winery's champagne capacity could fill 480,000 bottles. With the increased storage, the winery switched over to a newer system of producing champagne, the French Charmat process. This enabled it to make fine champagne but in a larger scale, and therefore it could lower the price of its champagne per bottle.

Kaiser Steel built a manufacturing plant in Fontana in 1942. This was a foreshadowing of what was to come for the wine industry in the Cucamonga Valley. The plant resulted in the removal of a significant amount of vineyard acreage for the construction of residences for workers at the new plant.

In 1945, Horace Lanza of Delano purchased a controlling interest in the Italian Vineyard company. Half of the stockholders sold their shares to Lanza with the encouragement of the board's president, Mr. Giulli. The other stockholders held out until the shares went to $1,550 per share. The company was renamed Garrett and Company.

GARRETT AND COMPANY

The story of Garrett and Company begins in 1835 in Medoc, North Carolina. This is the place where the first vineyard and winery were established by Dr. Frank Garrett. The white wine produced there was labelled "Virginia Dare" in honor of the first white girl born in America. The company produced wine in Medoc for fifty years and sold it direct to retailers. The company gained a reputation of producing a good wine, and the company grew.

In 1890, Captain Paul Garrett assumed control of the company as its president. Under Garrett's direction, the company grew rapidly. Sales of the Virginia Dare wine increased in different areas around the country, and Garrett concentrated on more efficient ways to transport the wine. A new winery was built in Weldon, North Carolina, next to a rail line. A branch plant was opened in 1900 in Memphis, Tennessee, as demand for the wine increased in the Midwest. In 1902, the plant moved to St. Louis, Missouri.

Garrett desired to increase the number of wines the company offered, so he began to purchase grapes from the California Wine Association, like grapes from Southern California regions such as Cucamonga. In 1911, Garrett and Company began leasing and eventually owned the Brookside Vineyard in Cucamonga. It opened the Virginia Dare Winery in the location of the old Mission Winery.

In 1913, Garrett and Company shipped its Cucamonga wine in specially designed glass-lined railroad cars to Brooklyn, New York. Each tank could hold five thousand gallons of wine, which was twice the normal amount being shipped of sixty to seventy barrels of wine. The special cars allowed wine to be shipped cheaper by five to eight cents per gallon as compared to shipping by barrel.

Garrett and Company began establishing vineyards in the Finger Lakes region of western New York, and champagne grapes were grown. Its headquarters had to be moved from Norfolk, Virginia, to Brooklyn due to state prohibition laws that had been enacted in Virginia.

Paul Garrett continued running the winery for fifty years until his death in 1940, at which time Howard C. Paulsen became the president.

In 1943, the company bought a winery and vineyard in Ukiah, California, and began creating table wines using grapes from that region. Finally, in 1945, the company bought the Italian Vineyard Company. Llewellyn Barden, who was the vice-president and general manager of Garrett and Company, moved his family from Brooklyn, New York, to Cucamonga to run the winery.

During World War II, the company assisted the U.S. government in the war effort. Wine byproducts were used as components in smokeless powder, synthetic rubber, parachute cloth, tents and medicines. "We lost one of the commodities that we used to import from France, Spain, and Italy which was Argoles. Argoles is the crystal that precipitates from the wine after the grapes are crushed, and it forms a crust on the wood of the tanks which is tartrates [cream of tartar]," explained Philo Biane. "These tartrates were used in the pharmaceutical industry for the production of remedies for burns. All of our wines that we used for distillation were first treated with calcium tartrate to precipitate the tartaric acid that was in the wine. That, in turn, would form the calcium tartrates that we were going to ship to the east coast to the pharmaceutical labs for the production of medicine. That was the variance that he had in production which was, in truth, our war effort."

Garrett and Company continued to expand and, by 1947, owned and operated three wineries and worked seven thousand acres of vineyards. Bottling was done in Cucamonga and New York, and the combined capacity was nine thousand cases of wine per day. By 1959, the company was offering forty-six varieties of wine and was able to store 4 million gallons of wine for aging.

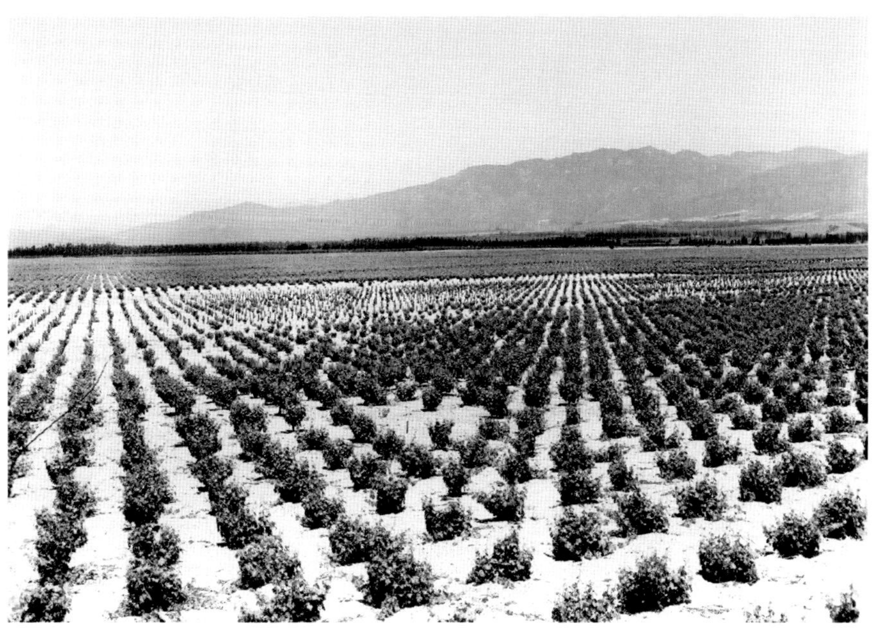

A young vineyard, showing the detrimental effects of how the wind hit in strips. *Cal Poly Special Collections.*

In 1961, the future of Garrett and Company and wine production in Cucamonga Valley seemed sunny. Because the land was situated in wide-open plains, though, the vineyards were often destroyed by the Santa Ana winds and wildfires. The winds would bury and destroy the vines with sand that could reach upward of eighty miles an hour. In a journal written by one of the foreman who worked at the vineyards, he wrote the following:

- *5-6-49 Sandstorm—The son of a bitch. There goes our bonus.*
- *5-7-49 Drizzle and Rain*
- *5-18-49 Drizzle and Rain. Field did not work*
- *Irrigating crew—Some drivers worked.*
- *5-28-49 Trace of Rain 3:00 AM*
- *6-3-49 Sandstorm appearing 7:00 AM*
- *Hope to hell will not reach here.*
- *6-6-49 Swallows returned to Guasti. Hope to hell Lorenzo doesn't destroy their nests. He always does—nuts!*
- *5-10-50 Sandstorm—Started 8:45 AM*
- *Field Crew worked all day*
- *5-17-50 Sulphur crew worked odd hours (started at night—stopped when weather was not permissible—resumed when conditions were ok.)*
- *Heavy drizzle—field crew worked.*
- *6-12-50 Received first shipment of grapes from Imperial Valley—to be crushed on 6-13-50 (Thompson Seedless)*

Wine production in the Cucamonga Valley progressively declined, but vineyards in Northern California were having high yields in their vineyards. For the many reasons mentioned throughout this book, the whole industry collapsed.

The Guasti region originally encompassed thousands of acres of land, but today it is a relatively small area northeast of the Ontario/Los Angeles International Airport. The Guasti ranch property, located just a few miles east of the primary winery facilities, eventually became part of the east parking lot of the Ontario Motor Speedway. Today, it's the western part of the Ontario Mills Mall.

Chapter 3

THE WOES OF PROHIBITION

During the mid- to late 1800s, there were few of the entertainment options that are available today. And medical, psychology and sociology studies were still quite underdeveloped. People did not know about the dangers of overconsumption of alcohol and alcoholism the way we understand them today, but what they did know was that the issue was growing. It was a complicated situation because it had both societal and religious implications.

In Indiana, circa 1816, society saw the first law on the books concerning prohibition of drinking alcohol, which is still on the books today. It prohibited the sale of any type of liquor on Sundays. The idea of controlling and even prohibiting the sale and use of alcohol grew, and by the mid-1840s, there were towns in Georgia, Indiana, Michigan, New Hampshire, New York and Ohio that had passed laws that made them "dry" cities. In 1851, the State of Maine passed a law that made it illegal to manufacture and sell liquor, and by 1855, there were another thirteen states that followed Maine's lead (there were only thirty-one states that made up the United States at that time).

Many great things came out of the Industrial Revolution (1760–1840), as it allowed industries to grow and become mechanized. The brewing industry was no exception, as new mass-producing breweries and mass-marketing efforts led to the rise of numbers of saloons across the nation. Unfortunately, the market became so saturated that some saloon owners became involved in criminal activities such as gambling and prostitution.

There was little distinction between beer, liquor and even wine when it came to supporters of prohibition of liquor.

By 1880, states were taking a greater stand, as liquor was being touted as the great plague of modern society. Kansas went "dry" as a state by amending its constitution. Other states such as Iowa, Georgia, Oklahoma, Mississippi, North Carolina, Tennessee, West Virginia and Virginia soon followed Kansas's example. The laws in these states did not allow wineries to produce wine for local sale but did allow them to sell their product out of the state. Most wineries could not survive, as they needed to be able to sell in their local market.

What is often referred to as Prohibition officially began in 1920. It was a constitutional ban on the production, importation, transportation and sale of alcoholic products. The feelings of Prohibition supporters were that the many ills that faced society were due to the consumption of alcohol. Those who supported the concept of Prohibition, referred to as "drys," were mostly made up of rural Protestants and social Progressives in both the Democratic and Republican Parties. Their influence grew on a national scale through the Woman's Christian Temperance Union and the Anti-Saloon League. Some of the drys went so far as to remove the mention of wine in school and college texts, including Roman and Greek classic literature. Medicinal wines were removed from United States pharmacopoeia. Some drys even went as far as to suggest that any reference to wine in the Bible was referring to unfermented grape juice.

Prohibition began to be enforced from state to state until it was passed as the Eighteenth Amendment to the U.S. Constitution in 1919. It was ratified by forty-five states in 1919, but New Jersey held out until 1922 and Rhode Island and Connecticut rejected it outright.

This amendment allowed for legislation to be created, called the Volstead Act, that enforced the banning of certain types of alcoholic beverages. There were two holes in this legislation that allowed the Cucamonga wine industry to not just thrive but grow. First, the act permitted the private ownership and consumption of alcohol, allowing persons to make their own "home wine" (up to 200 gallons per year) for their private consumption. They could not sell or transport it, but they could make and drink it within their own family (and, as a stretch, with friends). The number of home winemakers during Prohibition grew in epic proportions. Home winemaking production before Prohibition was an estimated 4 million gallons but grew to 90 million gallons by 1925, right in the middle of the Prohibition years.

The second gap in the legislation was the permitted use of wine for religious and medicinal purposes. In Cucamonga, a number of the existing wineries created medicinal and altar wines. They also produced other grape products, but one of the biggest industries was the growing of grapes for home winemakers, especially in the eastern United States. Millions of tons of grapes were harvested and shipped fresh to the East by rail.

Cucamonga was truly *the* grape and wine empire of the times. The red grapes grown in the Cucamonga Valley, primarily Zinfandel, became the choice of many home winemakers because the dry-farmed grapes had a thick skin and high sugar levels and shipped well. When Prohibition began, Cucamonga was producing more wine grapes than Napa and Sonoma Counties combined.

The demand for fresh winemaking grapes resulted in a shortage of refrigerated boxcars, which in turn raised the prices of the grapes. Many growers shifted from traditional wine varietal grapes to table wine and grape juice varieties, such as Alicante Bouschet and Alacante Ganzin, as these shipped more easily.

When the repeal came for Prohibition, there were 35 million gallons of wine stored in California, and most of that wine was created during the years Prohibition was in effect. In fact, the number of acres of vineyards doubled from 1919 to 1926. This caused the land prices to skyrocket from $250 per acre to more than $2,500 per acre. This increase in the numbers of grapes actually caused a crash of the grape-growing industry in subsequent years.

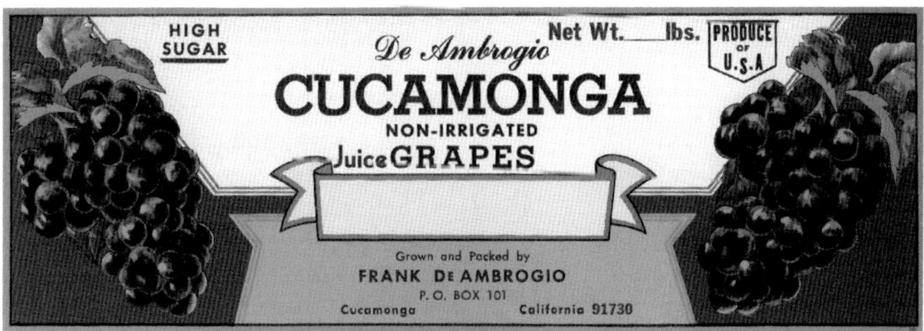

Grapes sent by rail were labelled "non-irrigated" juice grapes, denoting the greater sweetness of the grapes resulting from lack of regular watering. Grapes shipped to the East by rail was a huge business during Prohibition, as the selling of wine was illegal but the making and consuming of wine in the home was not. *Cal Poly Special Collections.*

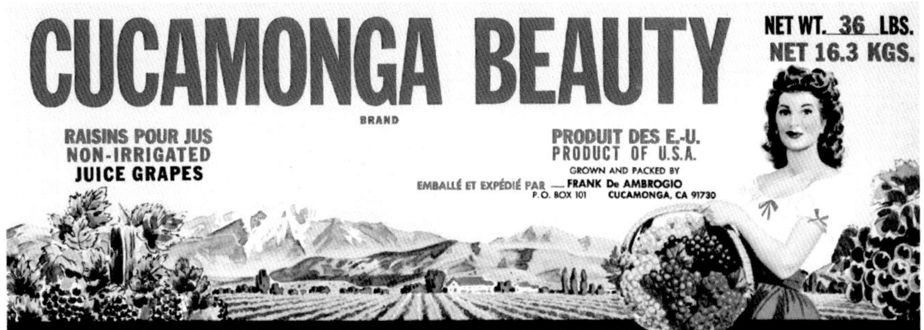

Grape crate label from Cucamonga that included information that the grapes were "non-irrigated." This meant the grapes were high in sugar. Grape clusters transported well by rail. These were excellent grapes for winemakers in the eastern United States, particularly prized by western and eastern European immigrants. *Cal Poly Special Collections.*

By 1925, there were more than enough refrigerated boxcars, so spoilage was less of a concern. However, too much fruit was now being shipped east, and the result was that grapes lay in great rotting heaps on docks. By 1926, land values in California had fallen back to $250 per acre, and a huge surplus of grapes in California exacerbated the problem. Part of the reason was that while the number of grapes being planted increased, the production of wine in California dropped by 94 percent between 1919 and 1925.

The Italian Vineyard Company had about 2.5 million gallons of wine in storage, the San Gabriel Winery had more than 1 million gallons and the Cucamonga Vintage Company had close to 500,000 gallons. Winegrowers prospered, while most other wineries seemed to be waiting out the storm of Prohibition.

Wine production continued during the dry years, as did vineyard expansion. Many vineyards doubled in size between 1920 and 1933. In the Cucamonga region, there were about thirty-five thousand acres of vineyard, and by 1925, there were about fifty-six thousand acres. Guasti's winery became famous for its grape concentrate, Vine-Glo. Many wineries—such as the Padre Winery (Vai Brothers), the Italian Vineyard Company, Garrett and Company and the San Gabriel Winery—grew and thrived after repeal, but many of the old wineries were lost forever.

REPEAL

Once repeal occurred, new winery ventures began in the Cucamonga area, such as the Cucamonga Pioneer Winery. It was a winery co-op, and it built a million-gallon winery. Also new to the scene was the Cucamonga Growers Cooperative, which produced about 500,000 gallons of wine annually.

In 1936, there were about 163 wineries in the southern region of California. Many of these wineries produced dry wines and fortified wines, along with sherries and ports. There were a few more experimental wineries like the California Kosher Wine Product Company in Ontario. In Claremont, there was a winery that produced an orange wine, while the Pure Honey Products Company in San Bernardino created honey wine (mead) and a champagne, as did the Padre Winery in Cucamonga. Muscat wines (Muscatel) had become popular, and many of the wineries were producing them.

A few years after repeal, the Cucamonga region was producing about 12 million gallons of wine annually, which was about 10 percent of the state's total amount. Even after Prohibition ended, many of the grape growers in the region continued to ship fresh grapes out east to home winemakers.

There were other challenges that the wine industry faced after repeal. For example, there had been a shift to planting inferior grape varietals due to spoilage issues of less hardy but more desirable vine types. Consumers' taste for wine had also changed. People were more in the market for gallons of cheaper "jug wine," sometimes referred to by the less culturally sensitive moniker "dago red." Americans had almost become accustomed to sweeter fortified wines. In 1935, 81 percent of California wines were sweet wines, whereas before Prohibition, dry table wines were outselling sweet wines three to one.

The French influence in the wine industry had all but vanished, and only two French wineries remained in California, one of which was Brookside Winery. There was a large migration of Italians from the East, and they began to dominate the wine industry in California, even to today. This is why there was so many Italian varietals being used rather than French. It was the Italians who really restarted the wine industry in California.

The most successful grape varietal from California has been the Zinfandel grape, which has its origins in Italy. The Zinfandel grape is black skinned and is still used in more than 10 percent of the wines from California. It was originally called Primitivo and was grown in the Apulia (heel region) of Italy. It made its way to the United States in the mid-1800s and was given the name Zinfandel, which is a name that probably has Austrian roots.

EMPIRE BEGINS TO VANISH

As was true for many industries throughout the United States, the Great Depression had a negative impact on the winemaking industry nationwide. It started in about 1928, which was still during Prohibition. Fruit Industries Ltd. enabled many of the families and workers involved in the wine industry to survive. "We were able to get along quite well," Philo Biane recalled. "However, those people that were not part of the operation had a hard time. They couldn't sell their products at that time, and they just went through a lot of misery." Some families had to do what they had to in order to survive, and the illegal business of bootlegging, or the selling of wine or spirits, became the only option for some.

WORLD WAR II

There was a whiplash effect caused by Prohibition that occurred at the beginning of World War II. The government wanted alcohol for the war effort, but there was not enough production capability because much of the grain used in distilleries was being sent for the war. It turned to the wine industry for help. As a result, the price of grapes went up, and the demand for wine and wine products increased.

"The federal government wanted part of our stills," Philo Biane explained. "Everything at that time was being directed towards the war effort. We were able to dismantle part of our distillery and had enough left for our own production needs. The other part that we had dismantled was given over to the government and re-assembled back in the grain area of the United States for the producing of alcohol for the war effort."

Only a few decades earlier, the Southern California wine industry had almost been completely wiped from the map due to the Anaheim disease, later called Pierce's disease. Although the industry had recovered and grown tremendously after this cataclysm, winegrowing in the Cucamonga/Guasti region now faced an even greater threat, one that continues to diminish grape growing in Cucamonga today: urban sprawl.

By the 1940s, there was a well-established agricultural industry in Cucamonga that included not only vineyards but also citrus, olives and other crops, as well as cattle. But now, people from the Los Angeles area were looking for new places to live and expand business. The Cucamonga area was beautiful and relatively untouched except for the acres of farms, vineyards and ranches. After World War II, people began moving east from Los Angeles, settling in and around the Cucamonga region. The vineyards were quickly being replaced with homes, buildings and asphalt. The price of land became too valuable to continue under vine, and many of the vineyard owners sold their lands for top dollar to developers.

As mentioned, in 1936 there were 163 wineries in California. By 1950, that number had been cut in half to 68 wineries. In all of San Bernardino County, which includes much of Cucamonga, there were 23,000 acres of vineyards remaining in 1960, but by 1970, only 13,000 acres remained; by 1997, there was just over 1,000 acres of vineyard left. In Los Angeles County, there were only about 29.6 acres of vineyard in 1997, and in the Anaheim region, no vineyards had survived at all.

Even though vineyards were shrinking, winemakers in Cucamonga held on strong. In 1939, Cucamonga had forty-one bonded wineries, thirteen brandy distilleries and storage for 13 million gallons of wine.

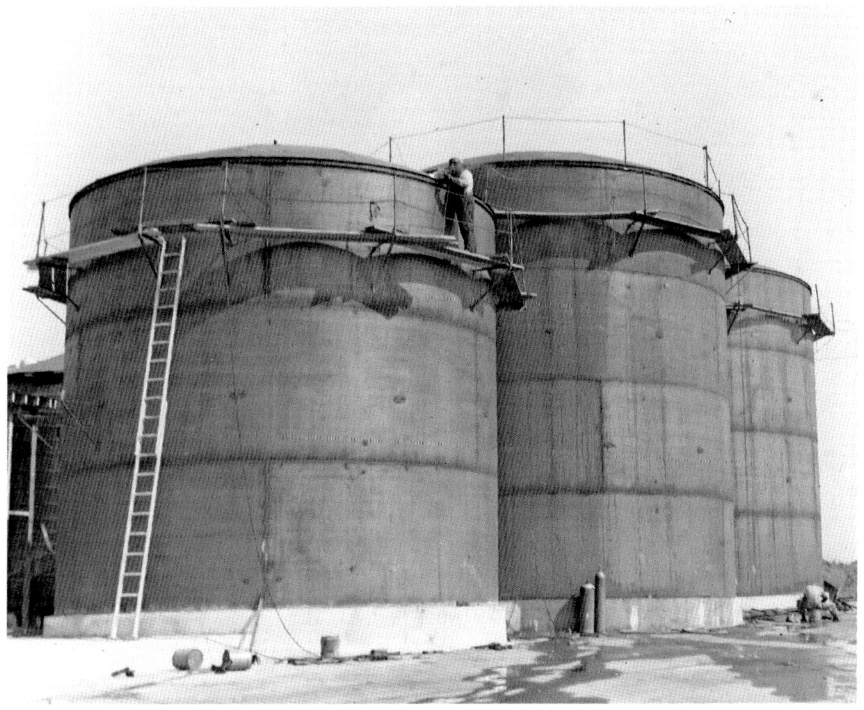

Outside storage tanks at Cucamonga Winery. *Cal Poly Special Collections.*

In the early 1940s, there were forty wineries and forty thousand acres of vines. This number actually grew to fifty-five wineries within the next few years. By 1946, Cucamonga was producing 12 million gallons of wine annually, but by 1950, that amount had lowered to only 7 million gallons. In 1960, the number of gallons of wine per year was still holding steady at 7 million. The wineries were then producing mostly table wines, which were popular. There were still sweet fortified wines, but people were drinking more dry table wines, and so the wineries continued to persevere a bit longer.

The one thing the Cucamonga Valley could not slow down was progress—the urban sprawl from Los Angeles and Orange County continued to gobble up the land. Resultantly, by 1970 the remaining wineries had begun to vanish. Agricultural land in the Cucamonga/Guasti region began to crumble under suburbanization, as there was more affordable housing options for families moving from the more expensive living in the Los Angeles and Orange County areas.

On the other hand, wine production in Northern California continued to grow and flourish, so much so that Cucamonga wineries could not compete, and so even more vineyard acreage and wineries were sold off. By the 1990s, there were only a few wineries that had survived. These still exist, albeit at a much-diminished scale today—Galleano, Joseph Filippi and the Philo Biane Winery.

Chapter 4

ACCOMAZZO

CUCAMONGA WINERY

Alfred Accomazzo and his family were from San Desiderio, in the Asti region of the Piedmont in Italy. When Alfred and his brother, Eduardo, arrived in California, they worked in various trades, including running their first bonded winery in Glendale, California, in 1916. Once Prohibition began, the brothers turned to real estate, but once repeal occurred, they were back into the wine business.

The Cucamonga Winery was built in 1933 by Alfred Accomazzo, who partnered with Dominic Merlo, Marie Pastrone and Louis Gotto, who sold his interest in 1935 to Joseph Ettor. It was the first winery that used the Cucamonga name, and they started with eighty thousand gallons of storage capacity. They bought 850 acres of vineyards throughout the Cucamonga Valley. They even had vineyards in other North Coast counties. In 1939, the winery was made into a California corporation.

Ettor had shipped grapes to the East during Prohibition, and he still had strong ties there that he used to distribute their wine after Prohibition. The Cucamonga wines were distributed in New York, Connecticut, Massachusetts, Vermont, Illinois and Ohio.

By 1950, Eduardo's son, Ed Accomazzo, had begun taking over the duties of the winery and eventually took over management. Ed served as a director of the Wine Institute from the late 1950s to the mid-1970s. In his retirement, Ed Accomazzo was in charge of the Cucamonga Vintners in Upland, California.

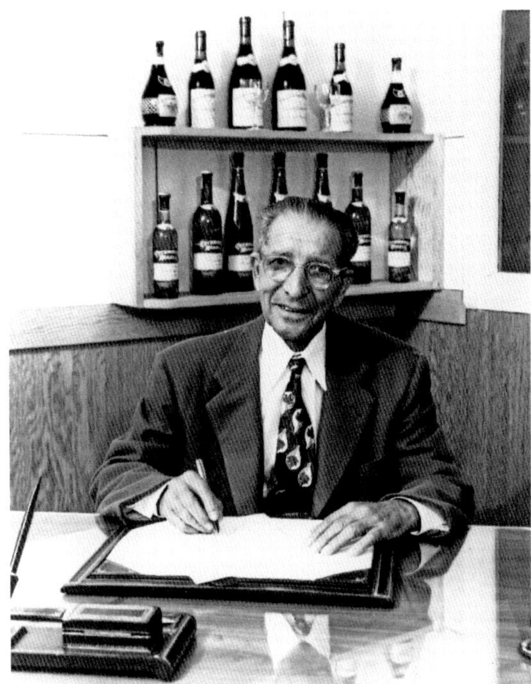

Left: Alfred Accomazzo. *Cal Poly Special Collections.*

Below: Transportation display, 17 East Forty-Fifth Street, New York, 1950s. *Cal Poly Special Collections.*

Opposite, top: The Accomazzo brothers together. *Cal Poly Special Collections.*

Opposite, bottom: Ed Accomazzo showing off grapes ready to harvest. *Cal Poly Special Collections.*

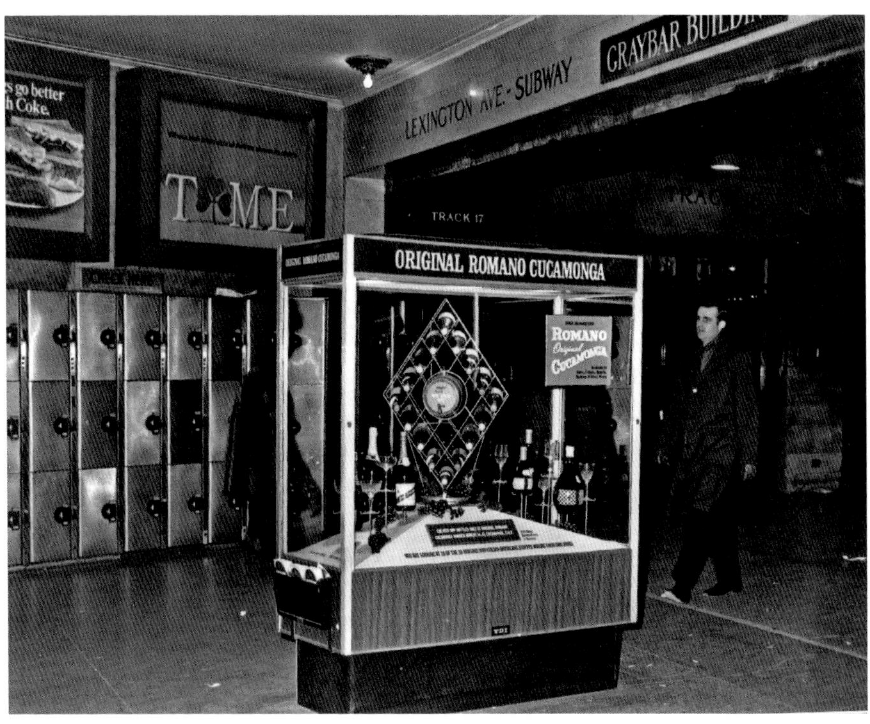

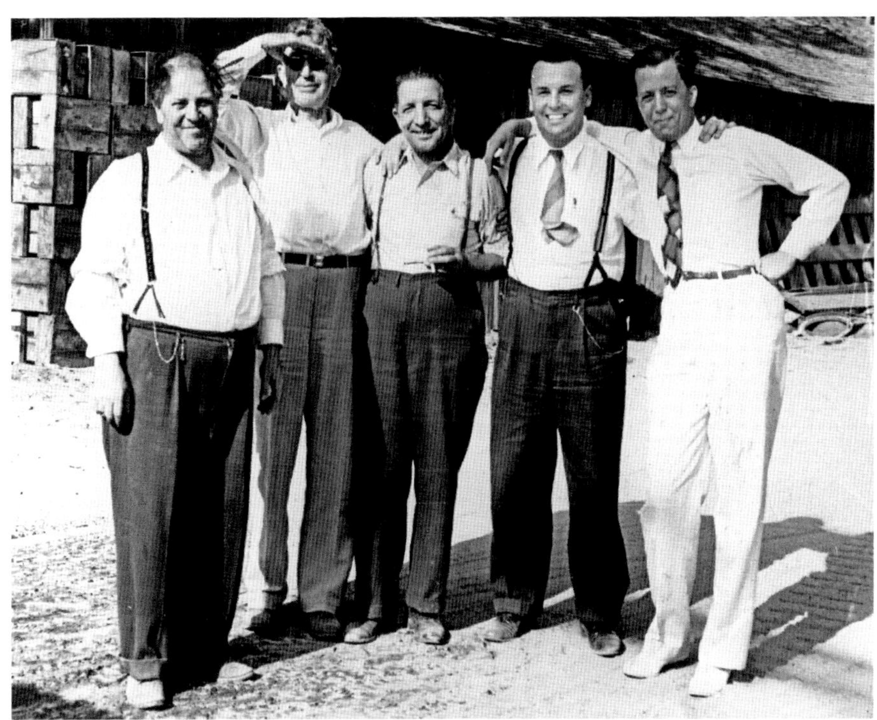

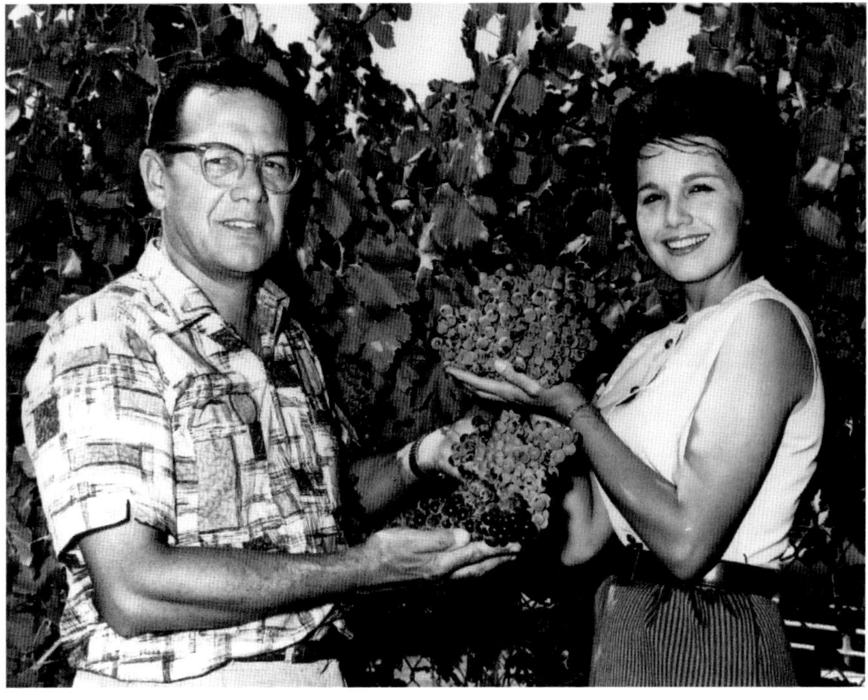

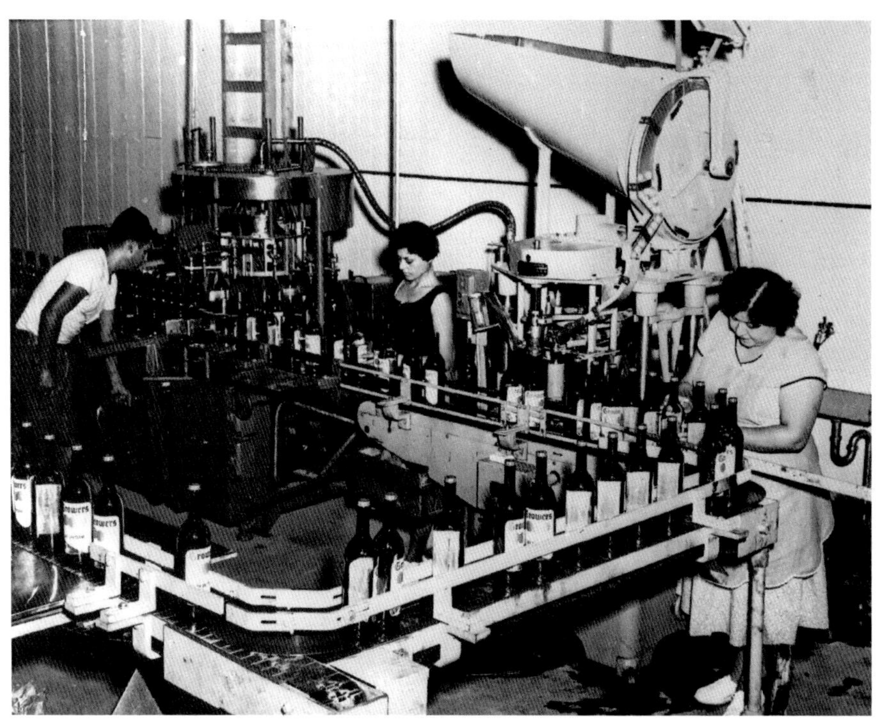

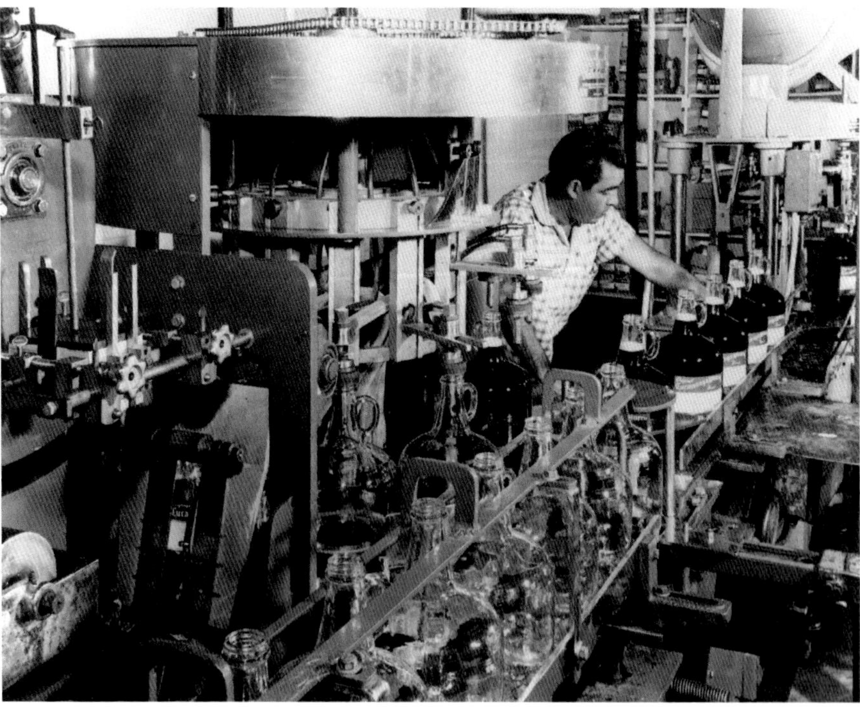

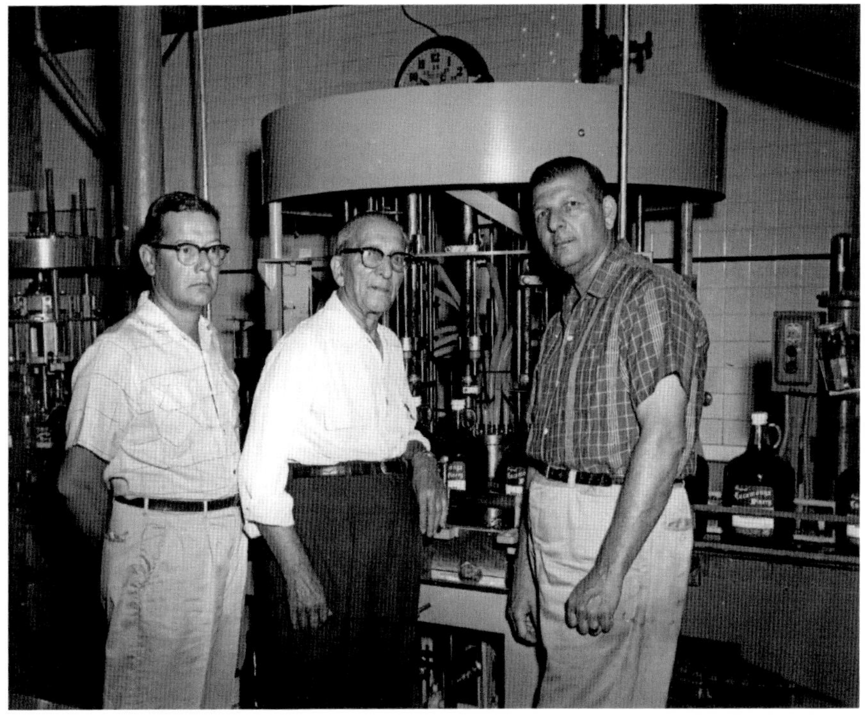

Above: Ed, Alfredo and Arthur Accomazzo. *Cal Poly Special Collections.*

Opposite, top: Bottling line at the Cucamonga Winery. *Cal Poly Special Collections.*

Opposite, bottom: Employee bottling jug wines at Cucamonga Winery. *Cal Poly Special Collections.*

Ed graduated from UCLA in 1938 with a degree in accounting. He spent five years in the military during World War II, and when he returned home, his uncle had asked him and his cousin Arthur to help with the winery. In 1960, Alfred Accomazzo passed away, and Arthur and Ed took over the winery as part of his family legacy. Even before Alfred died, they continued to expand the winery. They built a sixty-thousand-gallon cooling room to maintain storage temperatures between twenty and twenty-two degrees Fahrenheit.

The Accomazzo cousins also installed a semi-automatic bottle filler and new corking machine for the bottling line. They also built a combination fermenting and storage room with a capacity of 293,000 gallons of wine that was completed in 1951. When it was finished, the winery had

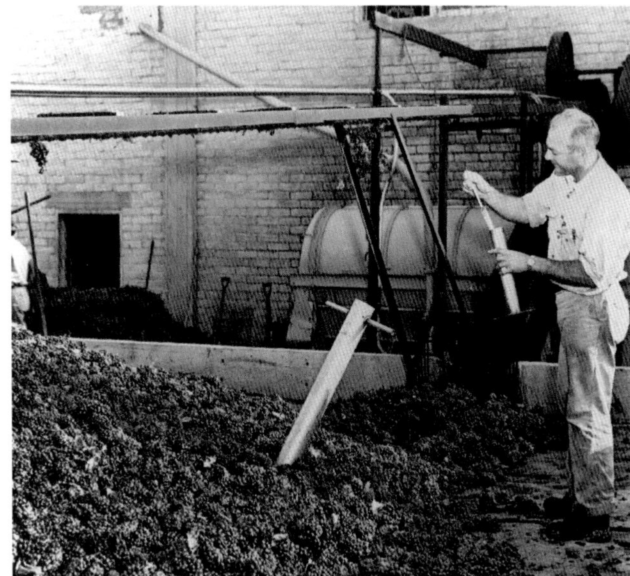

Winemaker Peter Smiderie, who worked as head winemaker from the 1950s to 1983, is pictured here testing the sweetness level of the grapes using a hydrometer. *Cal Poly Special Collections.*

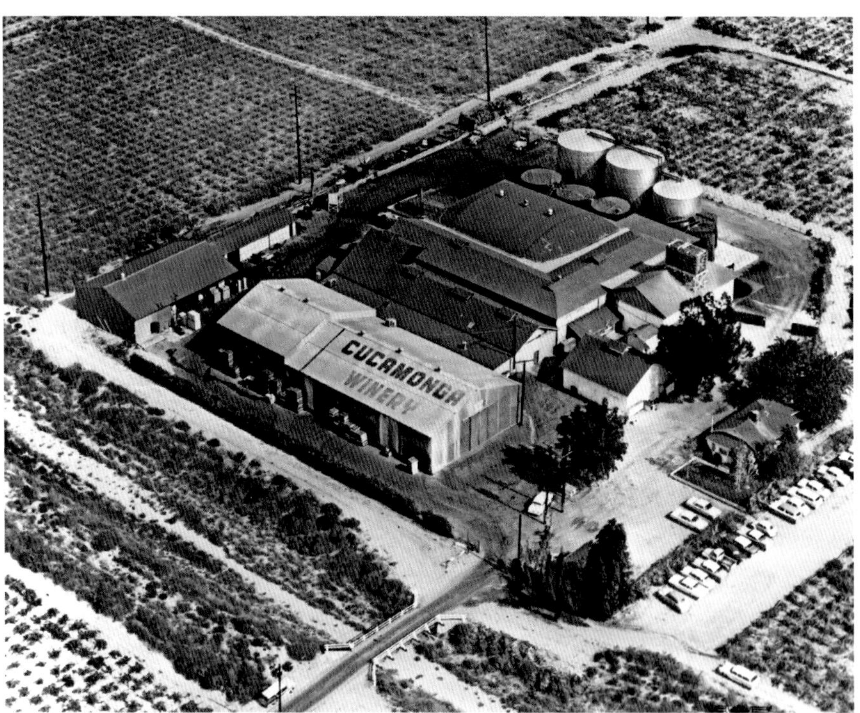

Sky shot of Cucamonga Winery. *Cal Poly Special Collections.*

a 1,293,000-gallon wine storage capacity. This included twenty-one steel tanks, two 87,000-gallon concrete tanks and a lot of wooden cooperage (barrels). In 1950, the company was cultivating 836 acres of vineyards.

BRACERO PROGRAM

There was a shortage of agricultural labor in the 1940s due to men going overseas during World War II. The Bracero Program was introduced in the United States in August 1942 as a migrant worker program with laborers from Mexico. The term *bracero* meant "manual laborer" or "one who works with their arms." It went into effect on August 4, 1942, when the United States signed the Mexican Farm Agreement with Mexico. The purpose of this agreement was to provide for labor camps that had decent sanitation, food, shelter and a minimum wage of thirty cents per hour to Mexican migrant workers. The program was continued through the Migrant Labor Agreement in 1951 and was finally added as an amendment to the Agricultural Act of 1949. The program was terminated in 1964. It was the largest foreign worker program in United States history, offering labor contracts to more than 5 million braceros in twenty-four states during its twenty-two years of existence.

The Bracero Program was run by a joint effort of the State Department, the Department of Labor and the Immigration and Naturalization Services under the Department of Justice. The program started slow, and only a few braceros were admitted the first few years through 1947—they only accounted for less than 10 percent of the U.S. labor force. Even with such low numbers, both U.S. and Mexican employers became dependent on the program. This led to some corruption through the use of bribes to get workers allowed in the program, and it also led to more undocumented workers coming across the border to work. Braceros became an important resource to the winemaking industry, especially in the Cucamonga region.

By 1951, there was talk of a new Bracero Program because while there was demand for more workers in the American agricultural industry, the problem with undocumented workers was on the rise. Mexico wanted stricter sanctions on American employers who hired undocumented workers.

President Truman signed Public Law 78 in July 1951, but it did not include sanctions. Shortly thereafter, a meeting between Mexico and the United States occurred to establish a new agreement in which the U.S. government

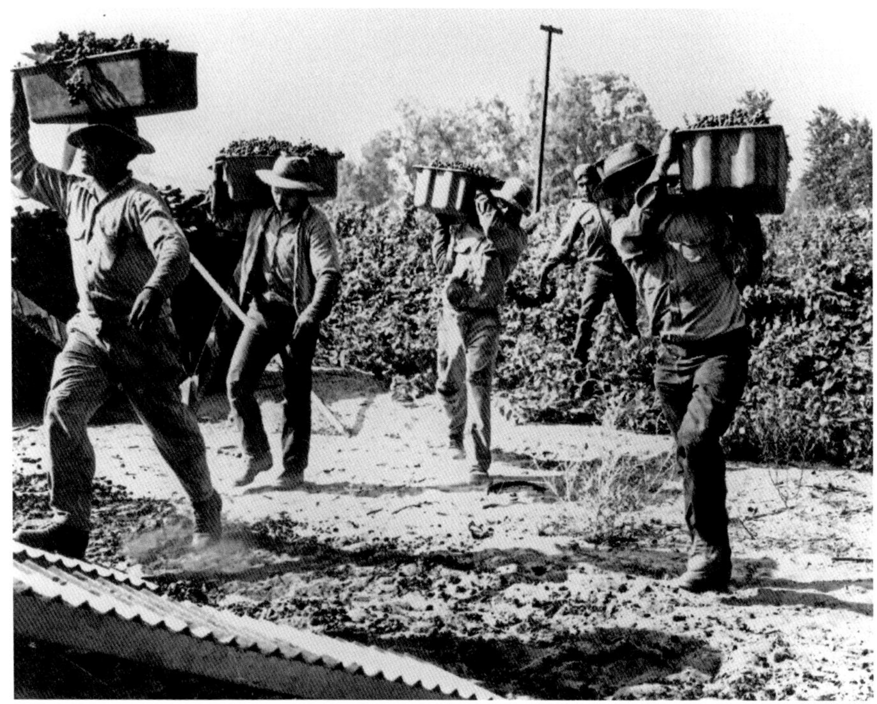

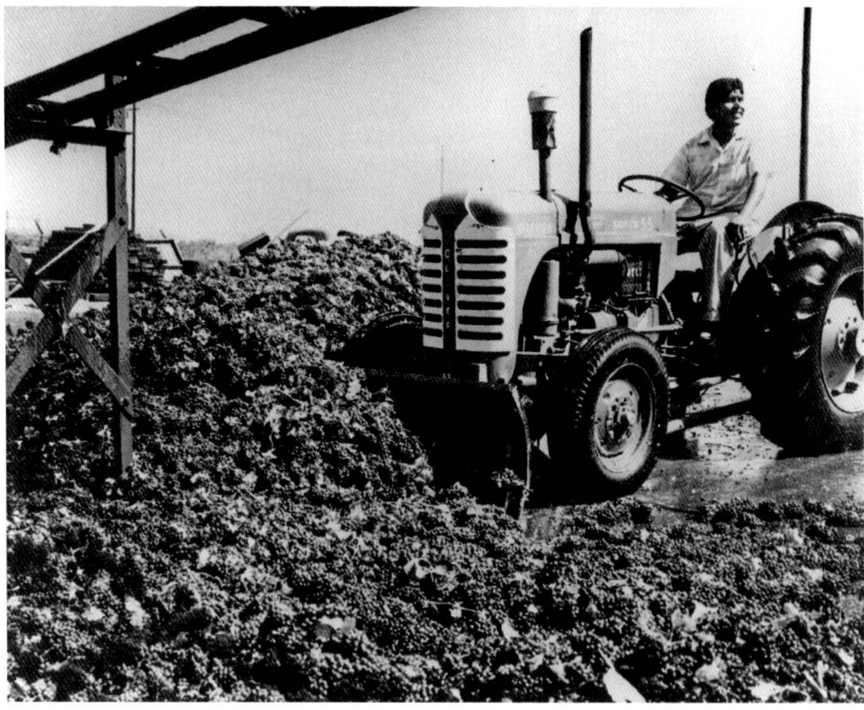

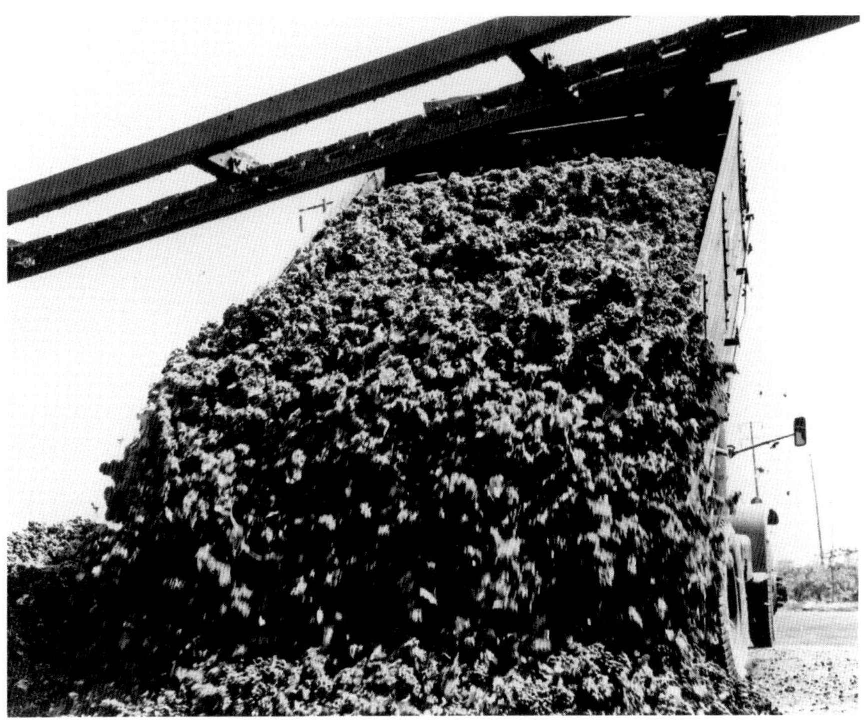

Above: Dumping grapes freshly picked from the fields at Cucamonga Winery. *Cal Poly Special Collections.*

Opposite, top: Bracero Program, imported Mexican labor. *Cal Poly Special Collections.*

Opposite, bottom: Employee at Cucamonga Winery on a tractor moving tons of grapes into the winery for crushing and destemming. *Cal Poly Special Collections.*

was the guarantor of labor contracts rather than the employers themselves. In addition, braceros could not be used as replacements during labor strikes in America and were not allowed to go on strike or be involved in collective bargaining on contracts.

In 1952, Congress approved a bill that deemed it a felony to harbor an illegal immigrant. This led to the H2 program in which laborers could apply for a temporary document to allow them to work in the United States. There was a lot of pushback about the new law and regulations, especially from labor unions, who stated that Mexican labor was harmful to U.S. workers. There were also complaints from others who argued that the process did not allow for enough laborers to enter the United States to work.

A new law was approved that streamlined the process by setting up reception centers at the U.S./Mexican border. Laborers were required to pass a number of examinations before being passed on to a regional migratory center. They were then required to pass a series of physical examinations, after which they were then allowed to move on to U.S. reception centers, where they were examined by health departments, sprayed with DDT and sent on to contractors seeking laborers.

In order to slow down the undocumented labor issue, the U.S. Immigration and Naturalization Service launched Operation Wetback in June 1954. It was not only illegal aliens coming across the border, but it was also laborers who stayed in the United States after their contracts had expired. More than 1 million laborers were sent back home during the operation's first year, and by the time the program ended, the number had risen to 3.8 million. Churches, farms and other concerned citizens were critical of the program. In 1957, several bracero centers were closed, and the number of workers in the program began to drop from 437,000 workers in 1959 to 186,000 in 1963. Although there were attempts extend the Bracero Program, it finally ended in 1964.

Ed Accomazzo was an army lieutenant in World War II. He was on the board of directors of the San Gabriel Valley Labor Association and was the director of the San Gabriel Labor Camp during the time the Bracero Program was active. He provided housing and food for the braceros. During an interview, Ed stated:

> *We learned a lesson. At first, they used to make sandwiches for the men. And they would take it out in a bag, but in order to make all of those sandwiches for that many men, they'd have to start at midnight making these sandwiches. Well, we soon learned that those sandwiches, by the time the men wanted to eat them at noon, were soggy and not very good. And they were throwing out most of the food. So, we came upon another idea which proved to be very successful. We'd line up all the makings of a sandwich in the morning as they had breakfast. The men would go through, have their breakfast, and then they'd go through the tables where there was all this meat, and sandwich material, everything was there. And we said, help yourself. Make as many sandwiches as you want. Which was a very good thing because they made the kind they liked, and secondly since they liked it, they didn't throw it away.*

There was controversy arising from the Bracero Program that is still being fought today. During the program, a 10 percent mandatory deduction from the braceros' income was supposed to be secured in an account and was supposed to be released to them once they returned to Mexico. Many braceros never received their savings deductions, and a number of lawsuits in the federal courts in California arose over the missing money. Many of the lawsuits were thrown out because the banks in which the money had been deposited existed only in Mexico, so the federal government had no jurisdiction. Legislation was eventually passed that the laborers who participated in the Bracero Program were to be compensated up to $3,500 for the mandatory 10 percent deduction. They had to prove that they were a part of the program and provide paystubs that showed the deductions. Today, it is estimated that ex-braceros are owed upward of $500 million in money owed to them, and they continue to fight for it.

The dissolution of the Bracero Program in 1964 marked the birth of the United Farm Workers and the shift of American migrant labor led by figures such as Cesar Chavez and Gilbert Padilla.

WINES PRODUCED

The Accomazzo winery was established for producing high-quality wines. The Romano brand of wine was named after one of its big distributors in New York. It was known for its wines, which were created with 100 percent Barbera grapes, considered the best Barbera wine in California in its time. The Barbera grape was, of course, an Italian grape, with a distinctive character that produced a flavored wine.

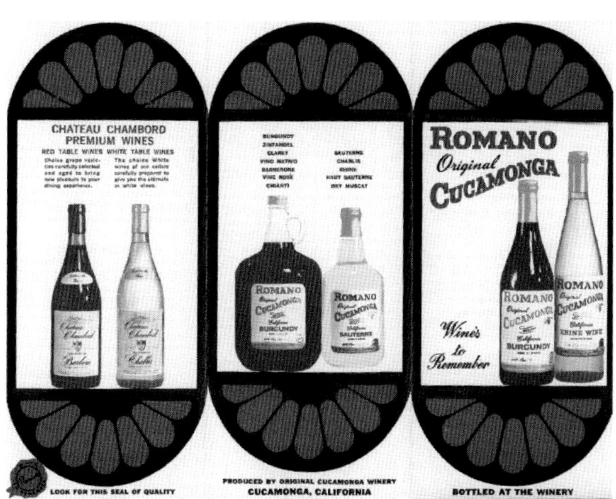

Brochure for Romano Wine, produced by Cucamonga Winery. *Cal Poly Special Collections.*

The winery also produced Zinfandel, Burgundy, Chianti, Grignolino, Claret, Barberone, Sauterne, Chablis, Rhine Wine, Dry Muscat and Vermouth.

The Chianti wines were bottled in a dark-green bottle with a squat shape that was common for this type of wine. It had red-and-white lettering painted on it and was considered to be light bodied with just enough acid to give it some depth.

It also produced a version of champagne. Arthur had been on a trip to the East and came back proclaiming there was a popular type of champagne called Cold Duck. It was a combination of red and white wine, which made it a pink color. Arthur convinced Ed that if they had some, they could sell it, and so they asked the Padre Winery to make some for them to sell.

Fighting Erosion

The winds of the region were extremely strong. Ed Accomazzo recalled an incident in which the wind tore off a roof:

> *In later years, instead of building a building, they allowed us to put tanks outside. Well, in putting those tanks outside we decided to cover them with a lean-to. Just a roof. But it was open on the sides, but we had a roof over it. Now our building was a kind of cone shaped building which made a nice air-foil. The big roof was made of two by sixteen rafters. I mean it was very heavy. One day the wind came along and picked up that roof, flew it over the building which was about fifty or sixty feet wide and landed it in our parking lot.*

A friend of the Accomazzos named Tom Carnesi came up with a way to try to fight the wind erosion, which was causing serious problems and reducing production. The worst winds would start coming in February. A plan was made to do all the pruning in January, so there would no cultivation until March. They created a Wind Erosion Committee in which the vineyard owners in the area participated. The idea was that during the winter, the rains would make the grass grow, and this held down the sand. Once you cultivated with a noble blade, you would leave all the prunings and the trash on top. This would create a wind barrier and keep the sand down.

WINE INSTITUTE

Ed Accomazzo was a director at the Wine Institute from the 1950s to the 1970s. It had four meetings a year, and representatives from all the wine regions met to discuss the wine industry and its future. They talked through problems they were having and would come up with solutions on how to solve them. One of the problems they had to work through was the shipping of wine to other states, as there were different regulations for each and some required a special stamp on the label. This made it difficult because they had to create a different label depending on where they shipped it. There was no conformity and consensus among the states.

In the 1950s, the Wine Institute decided to sponsor medical research into the benefits of wine. It released a report that noted that drinking a little white wine was good for a person's health, especially the elderly. This enabled organization to be able to introduce wine into hospitals to give to patients.

THE END OF AN ERA

It seemed the efforts of the vintners in the Cucamonga area would keep the wine empire alive. In the 1960s, Cucamonga was responsible for 98 percent of the 9.5 million gallons of wine that were being produced in Southern California, which included Los Angeles, Orange, Riverside, San Bernardino, San Diego and Santa Barbara Counties.

Even with their best efforts, the wine trade moved northward, and industrial winemaking began to grow in the San Joaquin Valley. Meanwhile, urban sprawl continued to devour acres of Cucamonga vineyards. By 1970, the acreage had been reduced to 11,400, which was the same acreage that had been used prior to Prohibition. The empire had fallen. There was still a lot of land, but the price per acre and taxes on that land had inflated. The land in the 1970s had grown in some places to $50,000 per acre, and homes were in the $400,000 range.

In the 1960s, there was another environmental threat to the vineyards: smog. In the citrus groves, leaves were withering, and the Ponderosa Pines in the San Gabriel Mountains were beginning to die. Some believed it was smoke coming from the Kaiser steel plant. Others believed that it produced smog responsible for killing grapevines in the area.

"When I used to drive down in the morning to our facility, I was driving east looking right at the Kaiser facility," Ed Accomazzo recalled. "I'd see black smoke coming out of there, hitting the mountain and then circling around. There was a chemist hired by Kaiser to dispute that Kaiser smoke was doing damage to the grapes, but that it was the automobiles that were doing the damage with their gases. He [the chemist] came into our winery, and I said, 'Look! Don't tell me. I look down the street. I see the smoke. I see it hit the mountain. I see it coming around. It's got to be doing the damage.' 'No, no, Ed. It's the automobiles.' Maybe a year later, Kaiser was shut down because of a strike. We still had the problem, and I had to agree with him that it was the automobiles."

In order to determine how smog was affecting the vineyards in Cucamonga, an experiment was done by one of the local universities. The scientists and students built plastic greenhouses around sections of the twelve vines growing in Cucamonga to protect them with the cooperation and help of Ed Accomazzo. The air was filtered within the structures. After a year, the vines outside the greenhouses only yielded half as many grapes and had only four-fifths of the sugar of those protected in the greenhouses. They continued the experiment for three more years. "They produced more, had better color and bigger berries," Ed Accomazzo remembered. "Everything was better. There was a 40 percent increase in the experimental crop over the three-year period. And not just an increase—they were better quality."

"Smog affected the producing capacity of our wines," Philo Biane explained. "For example, the Pedro Xeminus and the Carrignan [grape varietals] were really susceptible to the smog. In fact, they died as the result of the smog. The rest of the vines went down to almost 50 percent of their normal production."

Children of winery owners were going to college and finding other careers outside the winegrowing industry. The rustic farm life was less appealing to the baby boomers and subsequent generations. It was a tough life and requires a love of wine and the land it is grown on. Vineyard owners were eventually forced to sell their land.

By 1967, the Accomazzo cousins had enlarged their vineyard to more than six hundred acres and had planted Ruby Claret vines. By 1971, they had begun dismantling the winery and were selling their grapes elsewhere. Ed did not encourage his sons to get into the business because he thought it was a hard life. He would tell his sons, "You don't want to be at the whim of the weather." It was common for Ed to wake up at 2:00 a.m. and put out smudge pots in the vineyard in the cold months to prevent the vines from freezing.

TAXED TO DEATH

The ever-increasing taxes on vineyards became too much for many of the vineyard owners to bear. Ed Accomazzo explained it: "If someone sold a piece of land for five thousand dollars an acre, then all of the vineyards were assessed at five thousand dollars an acre in taxes. There was thirty-eight thousand acres of vineyard here. We could sell the land for five thousand an acre, but that is what we were expected to pay in taxes."

The taxes forced many people to sell their vineyards. Eventually, in 1975, the Cucamonga Winery closed. The family continued with the help of their trusted winemaker, Peter Smiderle, to create wine with another winery in Lodi. They were able to use their Cucamonga labels, and they stopped production for good in 1983.

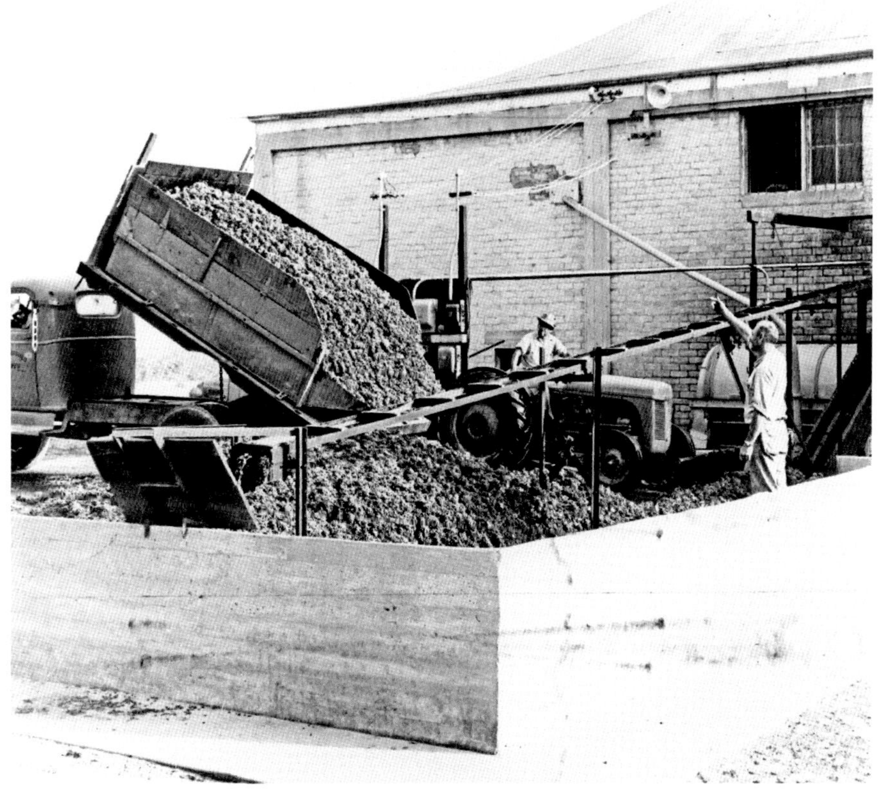

Processing grapes at Cucamonga Winery. Peter Smiderle is on the right. *Cal Poly Special Collections.*

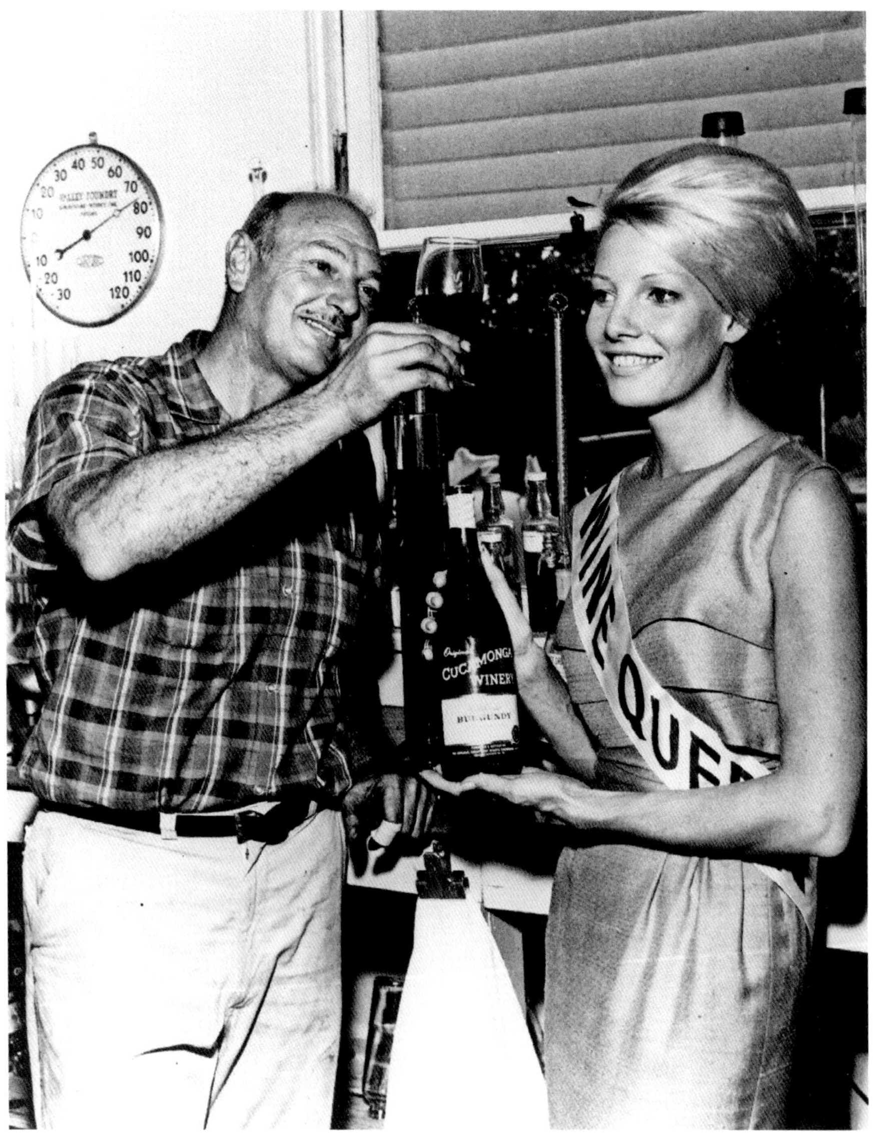

Smiderle and the Wine Queen, 1960s Grape Harvest Festival. *Cal Poly Special Collections.*

Peter Smiderle's son, Peter, has continued the family tradition of winemaking. He runs and operates the MoniClaire vineyard, named after his daughters, in Healdsburg, California. His intention is to continue the winemaking tradition of his father and his grandfather.

Chapter 5

FONTAINE CORAGLIOTTI

THE FOUNTAIN WINERY

The Fountain Winery was founded by Fontaine and Louise Coragliotti in 1934, opened in 1937 and operated continuously until 1970.

Fontaine Coragliotti was born on September 17, 1903, in Bosconero, Italy. His birth name was Defendente, but as a boy and young man, he used "Fantin" for short. In about 1930, he started using "Fountain" to make it easier for his American friends. Eventually, this became "Fontaine," which he used for the rest of his life.

Fontaine's parents were Mateo and Vittoria Coragliotti, and he was the youngest of three children. Mateo was on his way to California in 1903 when Fontaine was born. Mateo knew that Secondo Guasti had emigrated from Italy to America and started a winemaking region in California named after him. So, when Mateo arrived in America, he took a train from Ellis Island to Guasti and began working for the Italian Vineyard Company while saving money to send the rest of his family.

In 1912, at the age of nine, Fontaine immigrated to the United States by ship with his mother, sister and brother. From Ellis Island, they traveled to Guasti by train. They lived in a small house that the Italian Vineyard Company provided for its workers. Fontaine completed his education through the eighth grade at the small school in Guasti and then worked as a butcher at the Guasti Market.

Fontaine's parents were soon able to buy their own home, purchasing eighty acres northeast of Guasti in what is now Ontario. There was already a house on the property, and his father planted a vineyard on the remaining

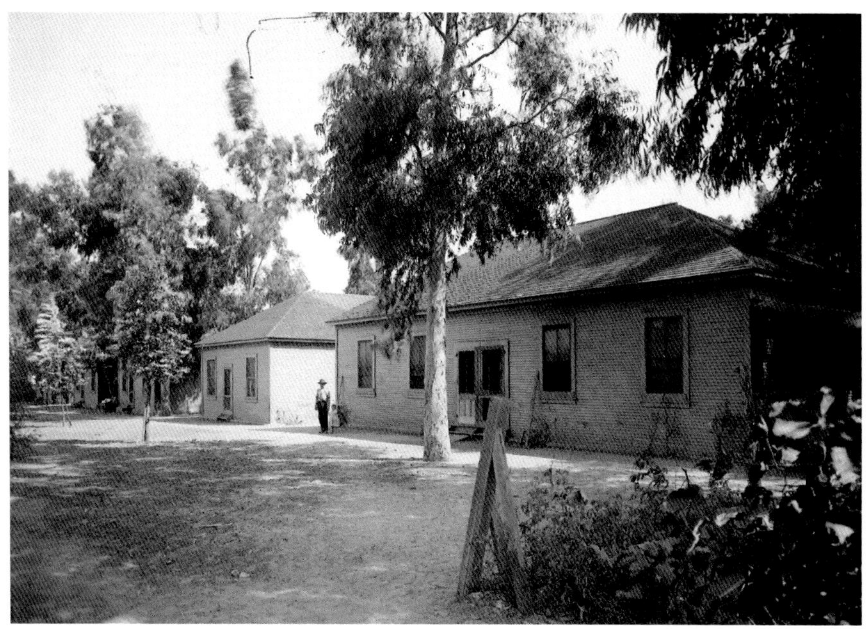

Homes built by the Guasti Company for its workers. These are larger than other houses and were for single men. *Cal Poly Special Collections.*

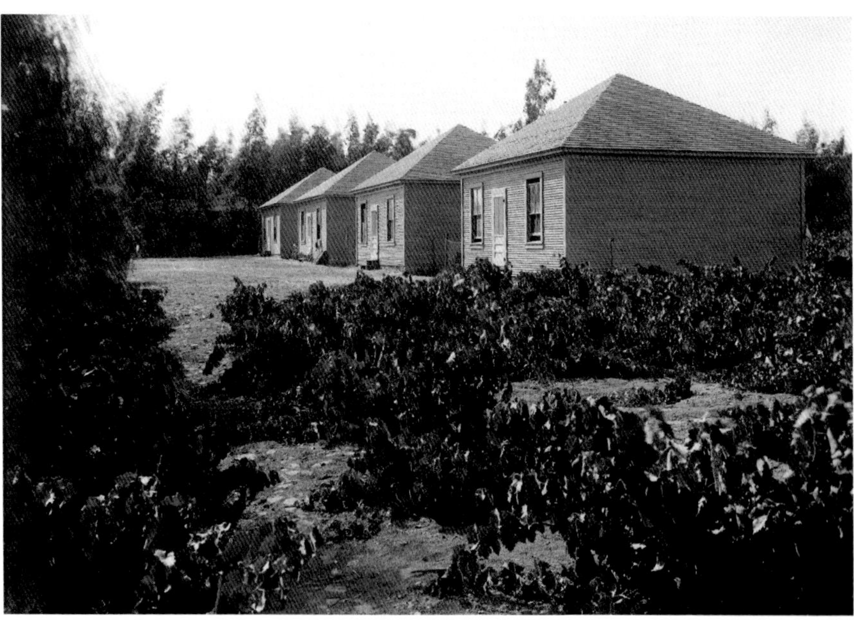

Guasti Colony company homes provided for married workers and their wives and families, 1914. *Cal Poly Special Collections.*

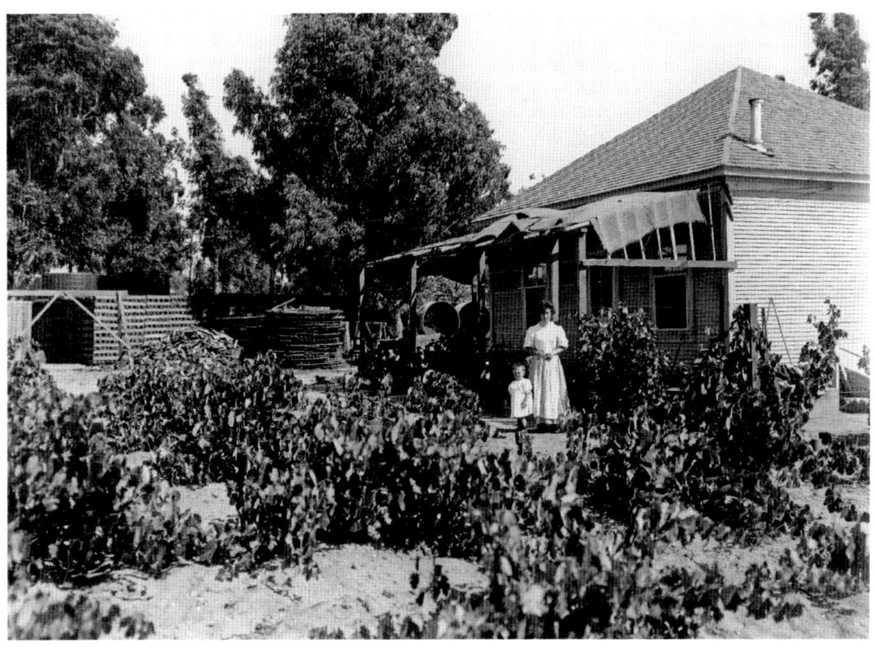

Woman and child standing in front of one of the houses of the colony. To the left is a pile of wooden stakes. *Cal Poly Special Collections.*

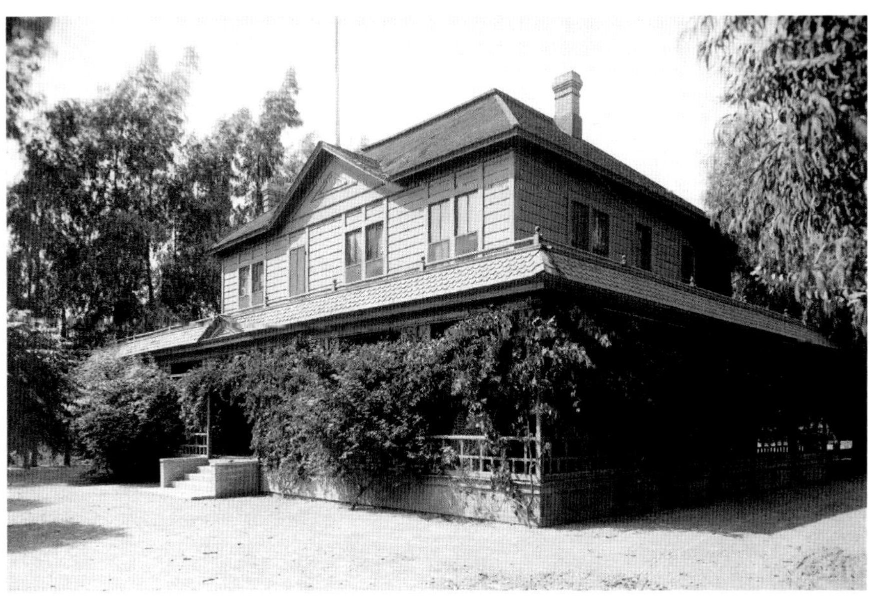

A view of the boardinghouse showing tree and shrubbery growth. *Cal Poly Special Collections.*

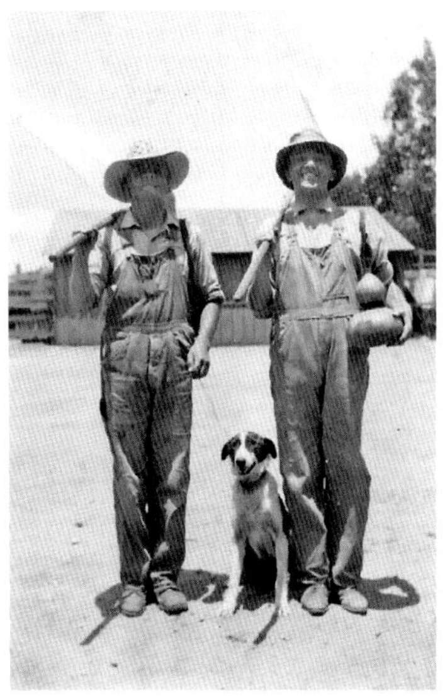

Fontaine with his brother Domenico at the Guasti ranch, circa 1927. *Mark Bianco Collection.*

land. Fontaine continued working as a butcher and helped in the vineyard when not working at the market.

Louise Gaggino, Fontaine's wife, was born on July 7, 1912, in Mombaruzzo, Italy. Louise's father, Carlo, left Italy for America in 1913, planning to send for his wife, Lucia, and Louise a few months later, but soon World War I began. They weren't able to follow until 1919, after the war had ended. From Ellis Island, they traveled to California by train, settling on a ranch Carlo had leased between Chino and Corona and growing wheat. Louise's younger sister, Mary Gaggino, was born in Corona in 1923. Louise completed her education through the eighth grade in 1927. During the busy summer months, she helped around the ranch and worked in Corona packing oranges and lemons during the winter.

Fontaine and Louise met at a dance in 1929. They were married in 1930 and lived with Fontaine's parents at their Guasti ranch. Their daughters, Betty and Helen, were born in 1931 and 1934. The family had outgrown the original home, so in the early 1930s, it was decided that Fontaine and Louise would stay in the original home with their daughters and Fontaine's parents would build a smaller home for themselves on the same property across the driveway.

Fontaine and Louise started a small winery in the barn on the property, making wine with grapes from his parents' vineyard. After a few years, they obtained a retail permit under the name Coragliotti Winery. There was also a small one-room building at the Guasti ranch. Fontaine's nephew Primo Scorsatto—Lucia (Coragliotti) Scorsatto and Frank Scorsatto's son—lived there for a few years in the mid-1930s, helping in the vineyard and learning winemaking. He married his wife, Rose (Battu) Scorsatto, in 1941. Primo would later become champagne master at the Cucamonga Vineyard Company. The one-bedroom building was later moved to the Holt Boulevard property for use as shed.

Fontaine and Louise continued to make wine and sell it to their friends during Prohibition, hiding it in a hole in the ground. The business was

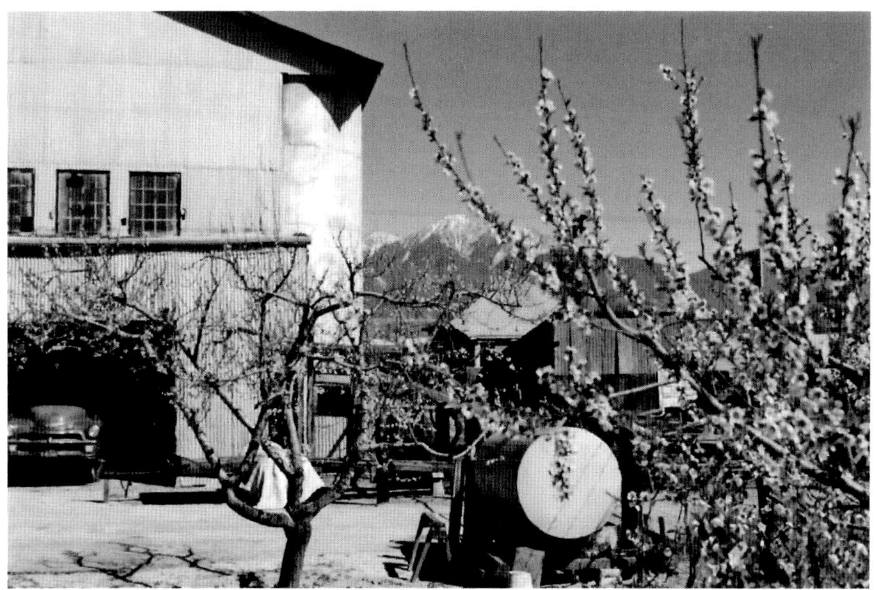

The south winery entrance to the silos, looking north, with the snow-capped Cucamonga Peak in the distance, 1970. *Mark Bianco Collection.*

successful, even though this was also during the Great Depression, and they were soon ready to expand. In 1934, they purchased property on Holt Boulevard in Ontario. There was an existing house and grain silo on the property, so they built their winery on the other side of a large driveway and then added a four-car garage south of the house in the mid-1940s. They moved into that house and opened Fountain Winery in 1937, California Bonded Winery no. 4253.

At the front of the winery building, which faced Holt Boulevard, was a liquor store from which they sold their wines and a variety of other products, including beer, liquor, cigars, cigarettes, candy and sodas. For a while, they also had a deli counter with cold cuts. Fontaine was the winemaker and businessman, and Louise kept the books. They both worked in the store during business hours.

As the business became successful, they needed more grapes to increase their wine production. They purchased an existing vineyard in what is now Bloomington and parcels of land in the local area as they became available. These parcels were generally grapefruit and orange groves, which they replaced with grapevines. They eventually had two hundred acres of vineyards.

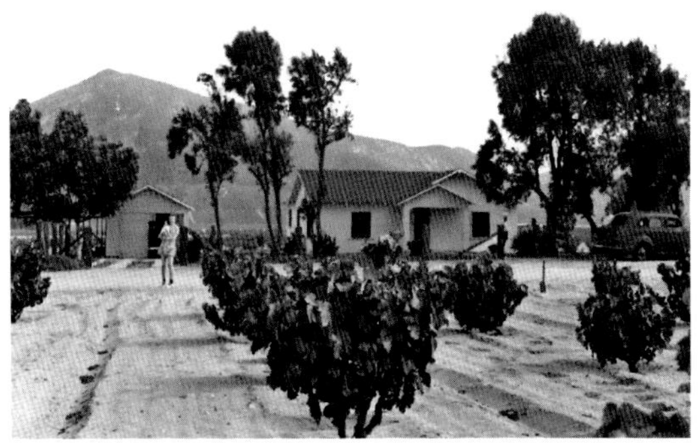

Bloomington vineyard, looking south, 1946. The people in this photograph lived in the rented home but did not work in the adjacent vineyards. The vineyards can be seen in the background extending up the Jurupa Hills. *Mark Bianco Collection.*

Not only were they successful as winemakers, but they also invested wisely in real estate and the stock market. They obtained the lots on either side of the winery property in 1945 and 1952 as they became available. In the mid-1930s, Fontaine and Louise had some money in a bank, but because of the many bank failures during the Great Depression, the banks would not give them cash for the full balance. Instead, the bank offered them either half of their balance in cash or a hotel that the bank owned due to a foreclosure that was worth the full amount. Fontaine and Louise chose the hotel, which became a successful investment until they sold it in 1975.

Looking forward to retiring after more than thirty years of running a successful business, Fontaine and Louise purchased a residential lot on Armsley Square in Ontario, a few miles west of the winery, and built their retirement home. They closed the winery and moved there in 1970. Over the next few years, they sold their remaining land and the Beverly Hotel. Fontaine passed away in 1974 at the age of seventy-one; Louise passed away in 1993 at the age of eighty-one.

The original address of the store and winery was 1250 East "A" Street. In 1956, the City of Ontario changed the street name and numbers, and the addresses became 1310 East Holt Boulevard (store and winery). In about 1945, the Coragliottis obtained the property to the west, at 1264 East Holt Boulevard, by swapping some land with the owners. They also purchased the property to the east, at 1316 East Holt Boulevard, when it became available in 1952. Both were used as rental properties, although Louise's father, Carlo, lived in the house to the west for a while.

In addition to the winery/store and house, there was a four-car garage and a large brick barbecue. Louise kept a garden adjacent to the garage and barbecue. They planted fruit trees (avocados, peaches, plums and apricots) and grapevines in the southern area of the property. They also leased the strip

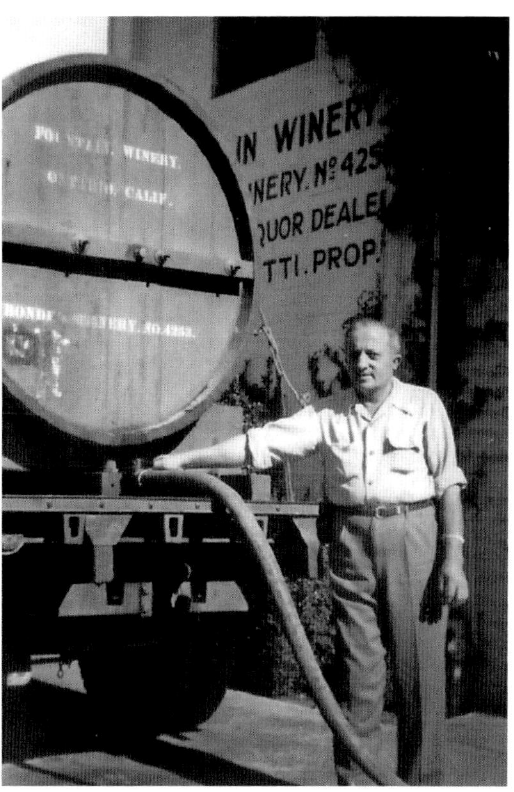

Right: Fountain Winery was founded by Fontaine and Louise Coragliotti in 1934, opened in 1937 and operated continuously until 1970. Its history was written by one of their grandsons, who remembered good times growing up with Grandma and Grandpa and playing in the winery on weekends with his sister and cousins. *Mark Bianco Collection.*

Below: Fontaine Coragliotti with his tank truck, 1947. It was used to deliver bulk wine to other Los Angeles–area wineries. *Mark Bianco Collection.*

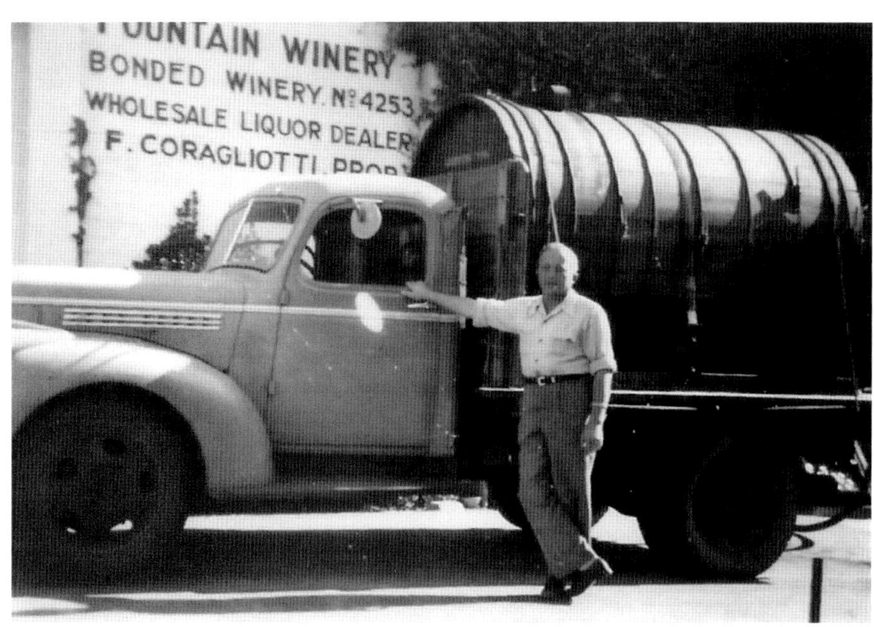

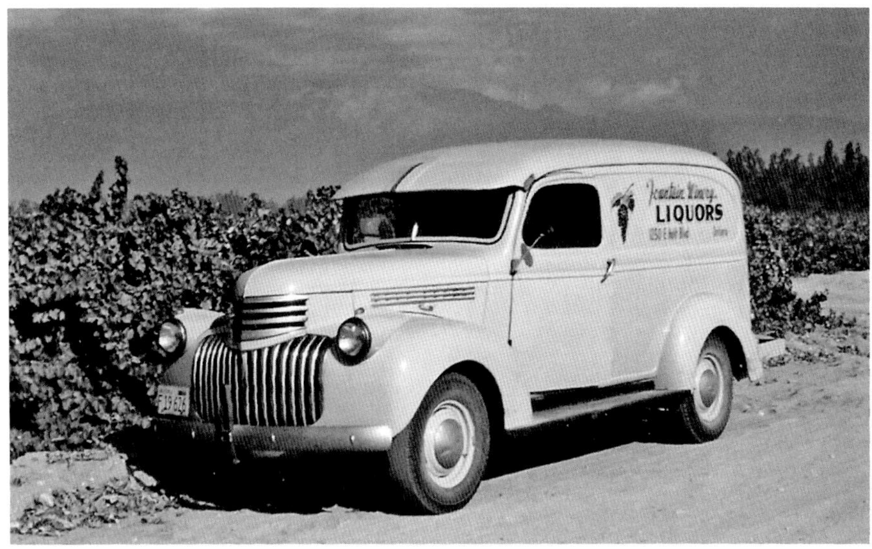

Fountain Winery delivery truck, late 1950s. *Mark Bianco Collection.*

of land between the south end of their property and the railroad tracks from Southern Pacific Railroad and planted more grapevines.

The winery was arranged such that the grapes entered the south end of the building, where they were crushed and destemmed. The redwood fermentation and storage tanks were at the center, and bottling, labeling and packaging took place at the north end just behind the store. Essentially, the grapes entered the south end of the building, and the finished wines were sold at the north end. The store consisted of a 480-square-foot salesroom in the center, with a 160-square-foot office to the east and a 160-square-foot kitchen to the west.

Fontaine and Louise lived in the residence across the driveway from the winery, which had a large basement. The southern half of the garage stored their personal vehicles, while the northern half stored beer and sodas for the store. Bottled wine was stored in the cooler winery building, and liquors were stored in the office area on the east side of the store. Candy, cigars and cigarettes were bought as needed from the nearby Smart and Final store. There was also a large underground fuel tank between the garage and winery, with a manually operated gravity-fed pump, to support their vehicles. At the south end of the driveway was a small one-room building (moved there from the Guasti ranch) under a large avocado tree that was used as a storage shed.

THE WINERY AND VINEYARDS

The original winery building was 3,200 square feet with a 16-foot ceiling and eight-inch-thick brick walls. At the north end, near the Shipping Department entrance, was a small loft area used as a laboratory for grape and wine testing. Bottling, labeling and packaging took place just inside the Shipping Department door and included a sink for cleaning and sanitizing the bottles. In 1939, the original winery building was extended an additional 1,200 square feet and attached to the silos, for a total of 4,400 square feet. The addition was attached to the south wall, and the existing large door allowed access to the new space. The south wall of the addition was built from corrugated galvanized iron panels to match the walls of the existing silo to which it was attached. The silos were never used for winery purposes.

The tanks were mounted on concrete pylons to facilitate cleaning between and underneath. There were two six-inch drains embedded in the floor on either side of center that ran the entire length of the building to facilitate cleaning. These were similar to the ones built in other wineries at the time, such as at Guasti.

The tanks ranged in size from 150-gallon puncheons (wooden barrels) to large tanks ranging from 1,000 to 6,000 gallons each. The large tanks were made from one-and-a-half-inch-thick redwood slats with reinforced steel bands. (Redwood is a neutral wood whose use was typical in those days.) The bottling station and basket press were mounted on wheels so they could be moved out of the way when not needed.

When the grapes arrived from the vineyards, they were brought to the crusher entrance, where the crusher/destemmer was located. The entrance was raised to facilitate unloading of the grapes from the trucks and trailers. The must (crushed grapes) would then be pumped to tanks in the adjoining winery building and then from tank to tank as it cleared and matured. A must pump and two sumps were located in the Fermentation Room to facilitate the transfer of must and wine throughout the winery. There was also a chiller in the Fermentation Room, mounted above the doorway into the main winery building. Wine would be pumped from its storage tank through the chiller with hoses and then back into the tank to control the wine's temperature and facilitate the clearing and maturing process. The winery did not have bulk storage for bottled wines, so they were bottled in smaller batches as needed throughout the year and stored near the Shipping Department entrance.

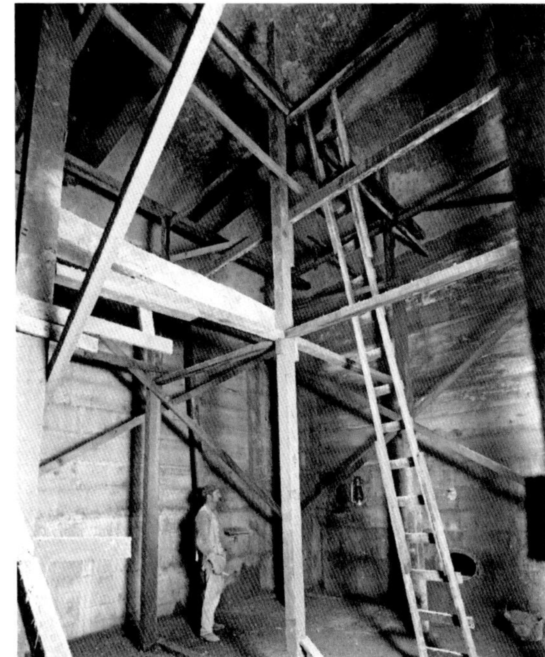

Left: Worker standing inside an unfinished cement tank. *Cal Poly Special Collections.*

Below: Construction of the two square forty-thousand-gallon cement tanks behind the fortifying room. The tanks were built by the Cahill Construction Company and were used to receive the crushed grapes for fermentation. *Cal Poly Special Collections.*

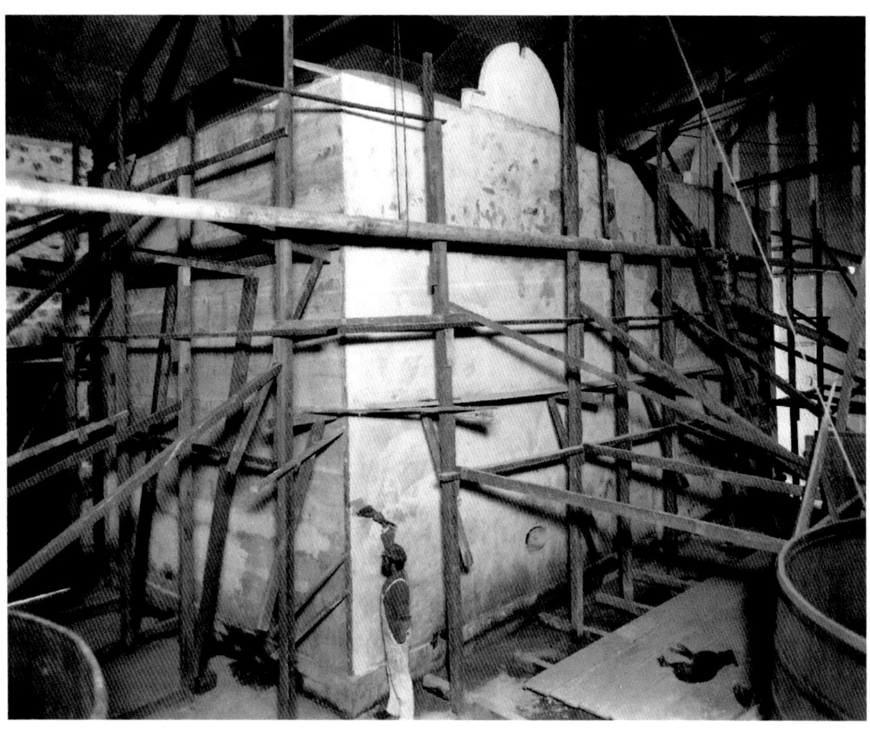

The wine was transferred from its storage tank to the bottling station with pumps and hoses and then plate filtered, bottled, labeled and packaged. Bottles were cleaned and sanitized with hot water and bleach in the nearby sink, and the labels and screw caps were attached by hand. The bottling station was on wheels and moved out of the way when not in use. Headspace in the tanks was purged with carbon dioxide (CO_2). None of the buildings was air conditioned.

The winery had the following fermentation and storage capacities over the years:

Year	*Fermentation*	*Storage*	*Notes*
1937	6,900 gallons in five tanks	12,500 gallons in sixteen tanks	The winery opened in 1937.
1939	6,900 gallons in five tanks	50,700 gallons in twenty-five tanks	Nine new storage tanks (38,200 gallons) were installed. The existing records are complete through 1939.
1956	19,000 gallons in six tanks	87,500 gallons; tank details are unknown	Some tanks were removed/ replaced and added between 1939 and 1956; the existing records are incomplete.
1964	8,000 gallons in four tanks	38,000 gallons; tank details are unknown	Some tanks were removed/ replaced and added between 1956 and 1964. The existing records are incomplete, but we know that at least eight tanks (37,500 gallons) were removed in 1964.

To allow Fontaine and Louise some time off, the store was closed on Sundays. (Liquor stores could not be open on Sundays during World War II, from 1939 to 1945.) In 1953, Helen's husband, Don Blasco, and Fontaine's nephew Primo Scorsatto started opening the store on Sundays, alternating between weeks. A few years later, Betty's husband, Enrico Bianco, and

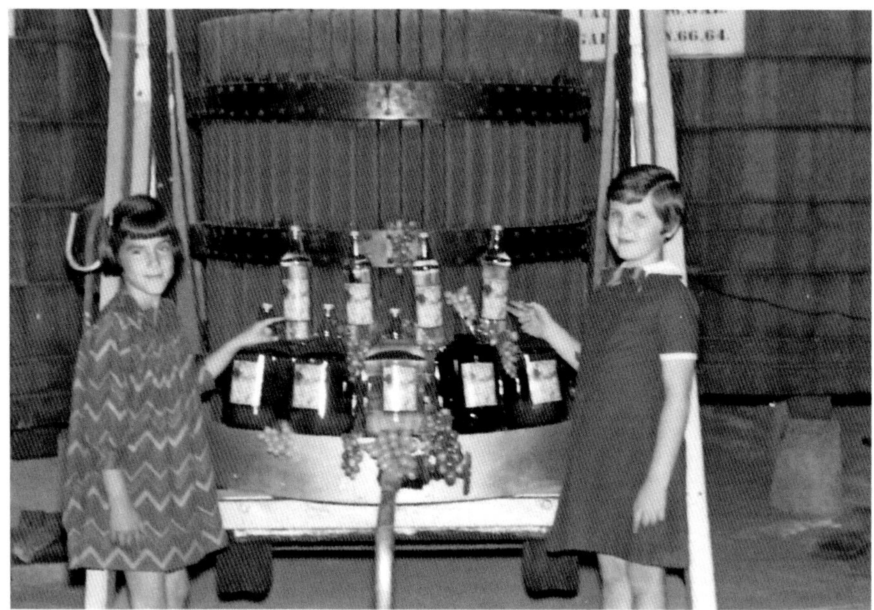

Basket press and storage tanks at Fountain Winery. The girls are Fontaine and Louise's granddaughters, Lynne Bianco and Cheryl Blasco, 1968. *Mark Bianco Collection.*

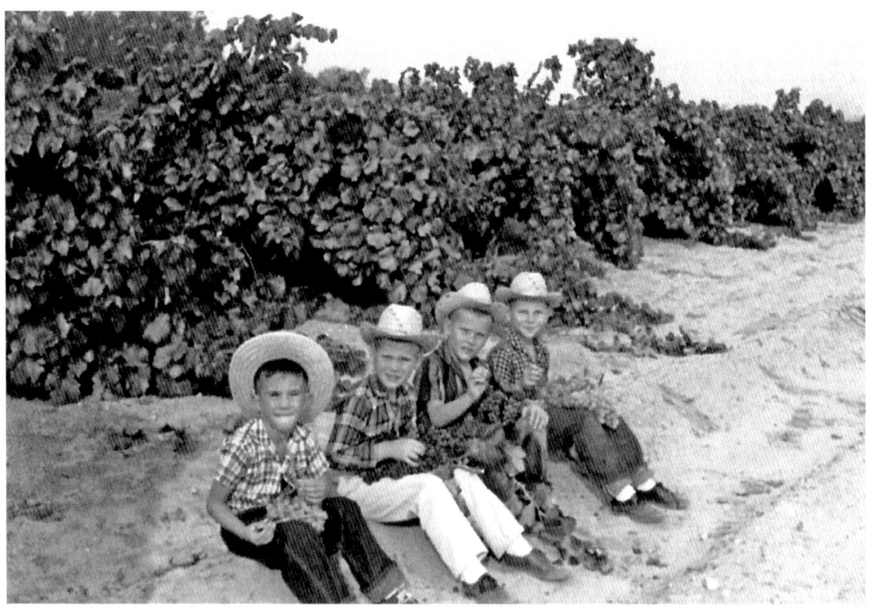

Fontaine and Louise's grandsons in one of their vineyards. *Left to right*: Mark Bianco and Eldon, Richard and Ronald Blasco, 1964. Note the head-trained vines and sandy soil. *Mark Bianco Collection.*

Louise's sister Mary's husband, George Davis, began working the store on weekends as well. Their children would play in the winery and adjacent grounds, and Louise would make dinner for everyone.

By the late 1960s, Fontaine and Louise had reduced their production in preparation for retirement. If they could get a good price for their grapes, they would sell them to local wineries instead of fermenting them themselves. If not, they would make wine with them. They also continued to bottle and sell their wines still in the tanks from previous years and operate the store as usual.

The winery's bond was terminated at Fontaine's request on April 30, 1970. Fontaine and Louise moved into their new home on Armsley Square and sold the remaining vineyard properties. There were no buyers for the facility as a winery, so the winery equipment was sold to a wholesaler in Los Angeles, and they leased the property to a small manufacturing company. In 1975, they sold all three parcels, which were sold again in 1977. Then Dietz Towing, which still occupies the site, purchased them in 1982. At some point between 1975 and 1982, there was a small fire at the southeast corner of the Fermenting Room. Damage was minimal, but the scarring can still be seen in the roof rafters.

The Coragliottis sold their 110-acre vineyard in Bloomington to the Southern Pacific Railroad in 1971. At the time, the railroad had advertised building a medical center, but this never happened. Today it's a combination of homes and warehouses.

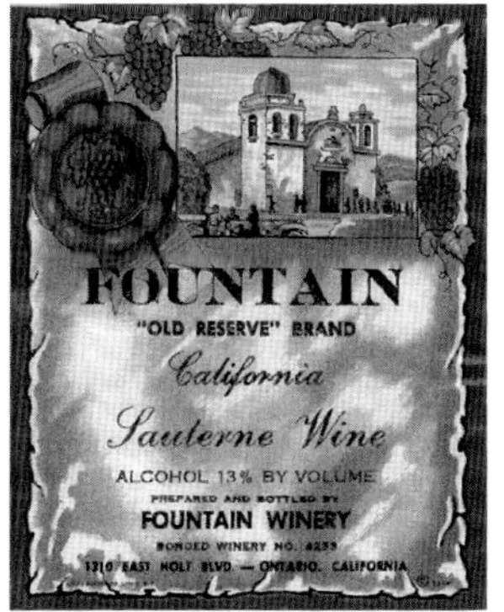

THE WINES

It is believed by the remaining family members, from their records, that the following wines were produced over the history of the winery: Claret, Sherry, Zinfandel, Tokay, Burgundy, White Port, Sauterne, Angelica, Light Muscat, Malvasia, Vin Rosé, Sweet Vermouth, Port, Dry Vermouth and Muscatel.

Original Fountain Winery label for five-year-old wines. Sometime between 1943 and 1959, the Coragliottis were told they could no longer use religious symbols on wine labels, so they removed the crosses from the "Old Reserve" label and the new labels were approved. *Mark Bianco Collection.*

Chapter 6

BIANE FAMILY

BROOKSIDE WINERY

The Biane Winery spans over five generations of winemakers in the Cucamonga area. Before he died, Philo Biane had been involved in the wine industry for more than sixty years.

There was a mass migration of French families who settled in Southern California in the early nineteenth century, with many of them fleeing the Napoleonic wars in France and Europe. When they settled in California, it was still under the rule of Spain; then Mexico took control, and eventually California became a part of the United States in the 1860s. There was a second influx of French immigrants to California in the 1880s in order to make fortunes in agriculture, especially the wine industry.

Theophile Vache, a native of the island of Oleron in France, immigrated to California via the Cape Horn passage in 1830. He planted vines south of Hollister in San Benito County in the "Vineyard District." Theophile's nephews—Emile, Theophile and Adolphe—came to join their uncle in America to help in the wine business. Theophile's brother, Alfred, stayed in France to tend to their winery and distillery there. Eventually, Uncle Theophile and Emile returned to France, but the younger Theophile and Adolphe remained, moved to southern California and established a wine wholesale business in Los Angeles.

In 1882, the Vache brothers established a wholesale wine, brandy and vinegar business in Old San Bernardino and leased a winery that Dr. Benjamin Barton had built there. In 1883, the brothers moved to Redlands Junction, ten miles southeast of San Bernardino, and it is here they built the

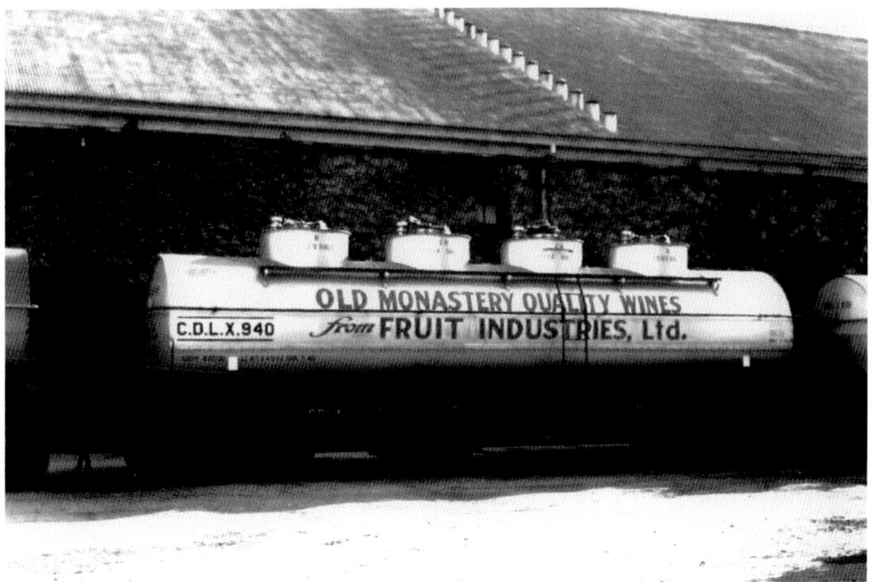

Railroad car at Brookside ready to transport fruit to home winemakers in the East. *Cal Poly Special Collections.*

first Brookside Winery. They purchased 400 acres of vineyard land in San Timoteo Canyon, and the winery was situated next to a creek, which gave Brookside its name. The Southern Pacific Railroad sold land for one dollar per 160 acres back then because it wanted to develop the land around its rail line.

The Vaches decided that it was a good area for grapes because the water flowing from the San Gabriel Mountains was pure. A number of water companies that supply water around the state of California have been successful because of water that flows through the foothills. They produced both red and white table wine, as well as brandy.

In 1892, Marius Biane arrived from his home in Gers, Germany, and began working for the Vache brothers at the Brookside Winery. Marius fell in love with Marcelline, Adolphe Vache's daughter, and they eventually married. He inherited Brookside and continued the tradition of winemaking at Brookside Winery. He bought some vineyard land in the Cucamonga area. In 1916, the winery was sold to Garrett and Company, but Marius Biane's sons continued to work for that company during Prohibition and eventually for Fruit Industries Ltd. (which eventually became known as the California Wine Association).

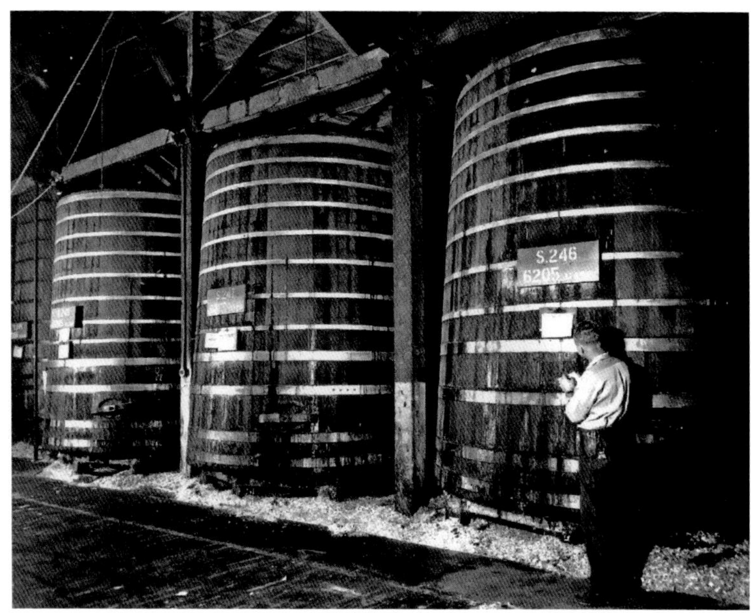

Winemaker checking tons of grapes fermenting in giant redwood tanks at the Brookside Winery. *Cal Poly Special Collections.*

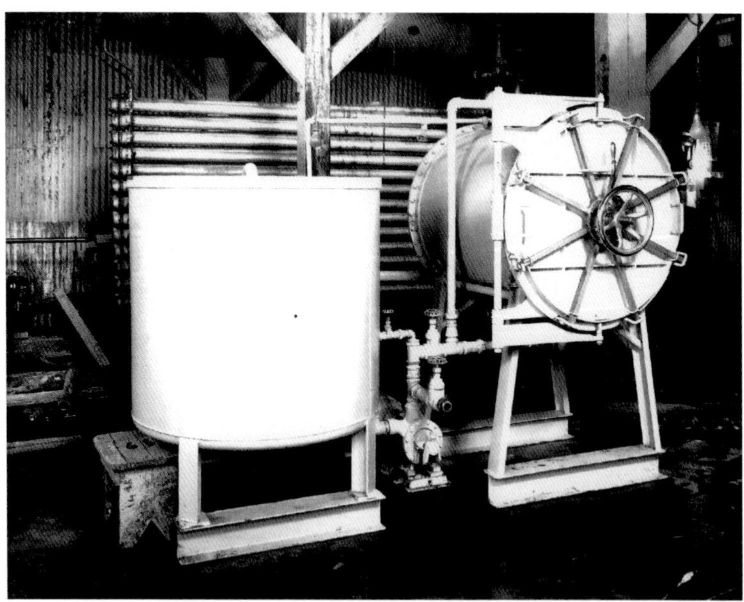

Winepress at Brookside Winery squeezes the new wine from the must after fermentation. *Cal Poly Special Collections.*

"Repeal was during the time of the Great Depression," remarked Michael Biane, Philo Biane's son. "It was also a time when Italian families moved from the east and settled in California."

Prior to Prohibition, the California wine industry was primarily French. There were about forty to fifty French wineries in California. In 1900, there were four French newspapers in Los Angeles. In addition to wine, the French were very influential in the baking industry, primarily bread, and the dairy industry. The area along the sea coast is still known for its sourdough French bread. "It is something about the humidity of the ocean which makes sourdough so good in that area," said Michael Biane.

During Prohibition, many of the French families sold their wineries and vineyards and immigrated back to France. "The families had made small fortunes with wine in the United States. Once they saw Prohibition beginning, they took their fortunes back home." The Bianes liquidated the Brookside Winery during Prohibition because while they could make wine, they could not sell or transport it. The Biane family moved to Santa Monica and lived there for about a year.

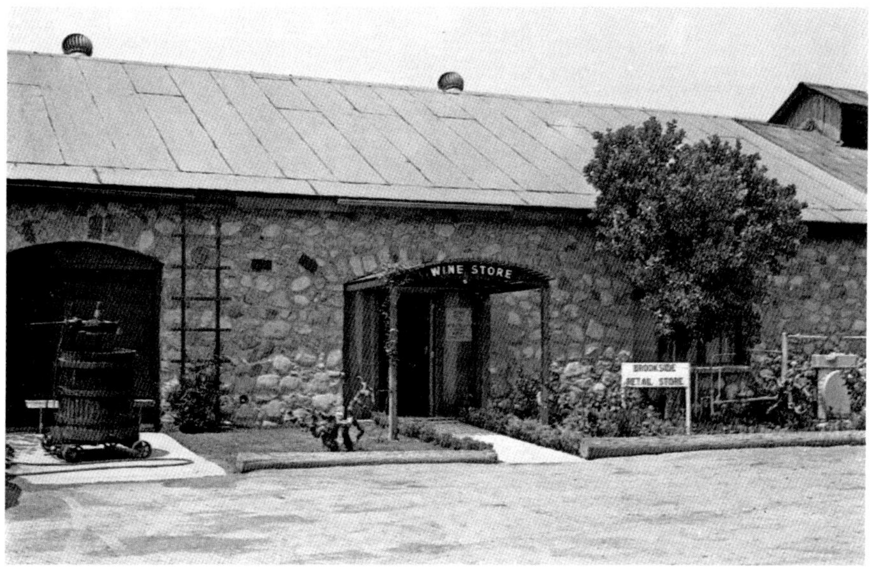

The wine store at Brookside Winery. It was the largest stone winery in California. Built in 1904, the cellars were six hundred feet long and one hundred feet wide, with walls three feet thick and twenty-three feet high. It was also had the largest underground cellar in the state of California. The winery was the scene of the annual wine festival held each fall. *Cal Poly Special Collections.*

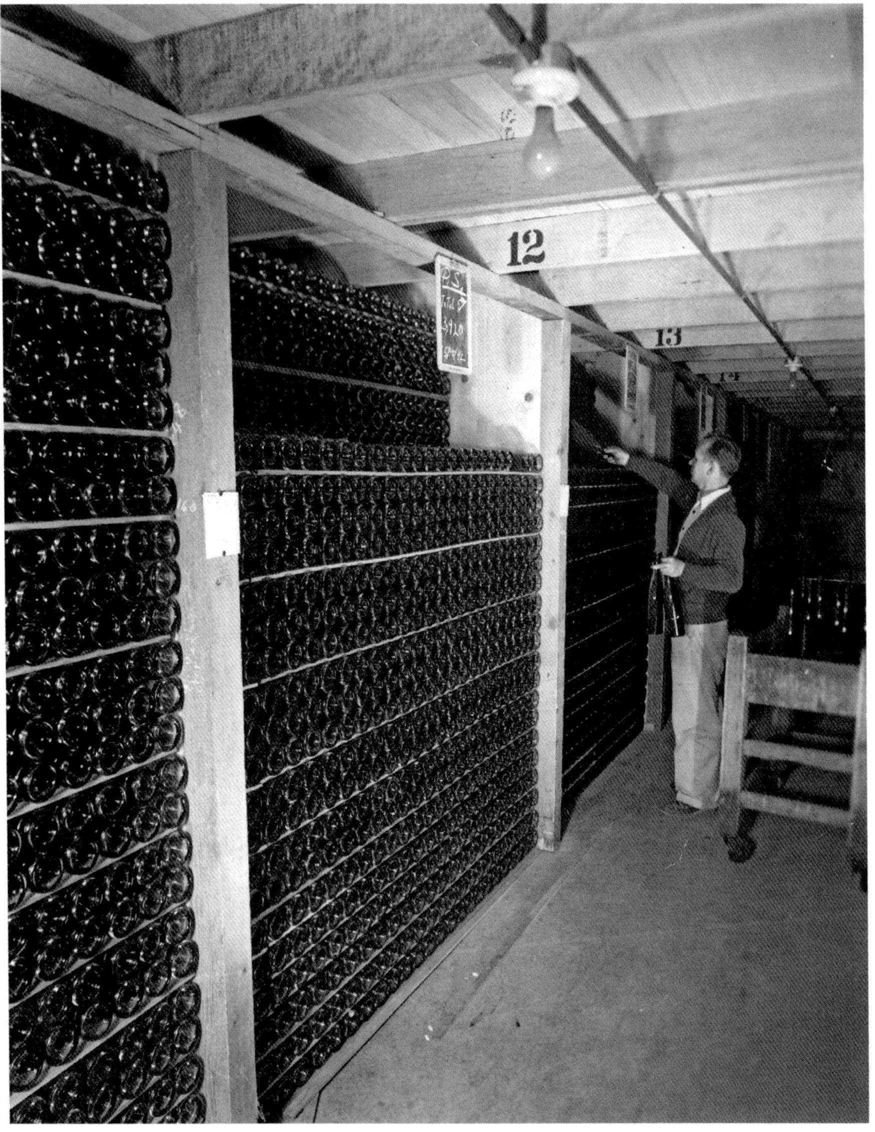

The cellars of the Brookside Winery held thousands of bottles of wine in controlled conditions. *Cal Poly Special Collections.*

One day, there was a knock on their screen door, and it was a man named John Klusman. He had made his fortune in the gold fields in Alaska and had returned to Cucamonga. Klusman wanted to build a vineyard, and he and his business partner, M.E. Post, wanted Marius to return and help them. Klusman was one of the owners of the Mission Vineyard company on Haven Avenue and Foothill Boulevard. It later became Virginia Dare Winery when Garrett and Company bought them out.

In addition to grapes, there was also a fruit and citrus industry. The fruit was mostly "stone" fruits such as apricots and peaches, along with the citrus fruits such as Navels, Valencias and grapefruit. The grapes had an advantage in that they had to be watered for the first year to become established, but then they could survive due to their tap roots digging deep to find water. The other fruit trees needed more care and more water. The grapes were grown in the foothills rather than in higher elevations due to the sandy soil.

In 1940, the Bianes purchased four hundred acres of land in South Ontario, and in 1952, the Biane family decided to resurrect the Brookside Vineyard Company winery, this time in Guasti. They purchased the Guasti plant that had been built in 1904 from the California Wine Association. It was built from stones mined from the mountains to the north. It had vast underground stone storage cellars, one of which was 20 feet underground and measured 175 feet long and 100 feet wide. In Cucamonga, Guasti's winery had buildings (Old Padre Winery) in which it produced the wine and then sent it to its facilities in Guasti for bottling and ageing.

THE FAMILY

Philo had four siblings: Francois (Pomp), Elenora (Sister Marceline), Phile (named after his Great-Uncle Theophile) and Hortense. Philo said in an interview for an oral history project in 1992:

> *I first became involved with grapes on my father's vineyard on Rochester Avenue in Cucamonga. Originally, the land had been vacant. It was then used primarily to raise types of corn, mostly milomaze for chicken feed and such. It was cut up into ten acre plots, from which Dad acquired approximately one hundred and sixty acres. Those plots were done on purpose for the problem of wind erosion in the area. Windbreaks of pepper trees had been planted every ten acres. This land had to be cleared of the windbreaks, and it also had a bad infestation of Johnson grass. This Johnson grass had to be literally dug out by hand in order to eradicate it. My first work was working with this Johnson grass. Later on, Dad planted the vineyard. My brother and I continued to work from time to time in the vineyard.*

The work was hard, and everyone in the family was required to help in the process:

> *The picking of grapes was, of course, seasonal. The season started in September and carried on through into November, or at least the first part of November. In the early part of the season we'd allow youngsters to work in the field picking grapes before their school started. We had about three to four weeks that we could work in the fields before going to school. Picking was done by hand using a curved knife to cut the stem, and then the grapes were placed in fifty pound boxes.*
>
> *It was difficult for the women and the younger boys to maneuver these heavy boxes from vine to vine, and then finally stack them at the end of the row. My brother and I worked in the fields picking grapes. We used a stretcher device that allowed us to put the box in the middle so that we could pick it up from both ends and carry it out to the roadways.*
>
> *At that point, the grape boxes were stacked and checked off by an employee called a "checker." We had a card and he punched the number of boxes that we'd picked for that particular row. At the end of the day, these were added up and marked with a name as having picked that many boxes. As I remember, the price was five cents per fifty-pound box of grapes. The boxes were loaded onto a wagon and pulled by a team of horses or mules and ultimately conveyed to the winery for crushing. We could pick probably forty or fifty of the fifty pound boxes in a day.*

This was during a time when automobiles were still new and very expensive. The vineyard was worked using horses and mules:

> *The animals were used completely for the cultivation of the crops. In the vineyards, we used a small plow to turn the soil, and then a cultivator to keep the soil loose so that the sun wouldn't penetrate. We did that way up into July because the mules could pass through the vineyards without hurting the vines.*

The original buildings that Guasti had built and then were used by the Biane family still stand today in a fenced-off abandoned lot, waiting to be moved or destroyed with future development. Even though the winery buildings were made of stone, the houses were, intentionally, not built to last:

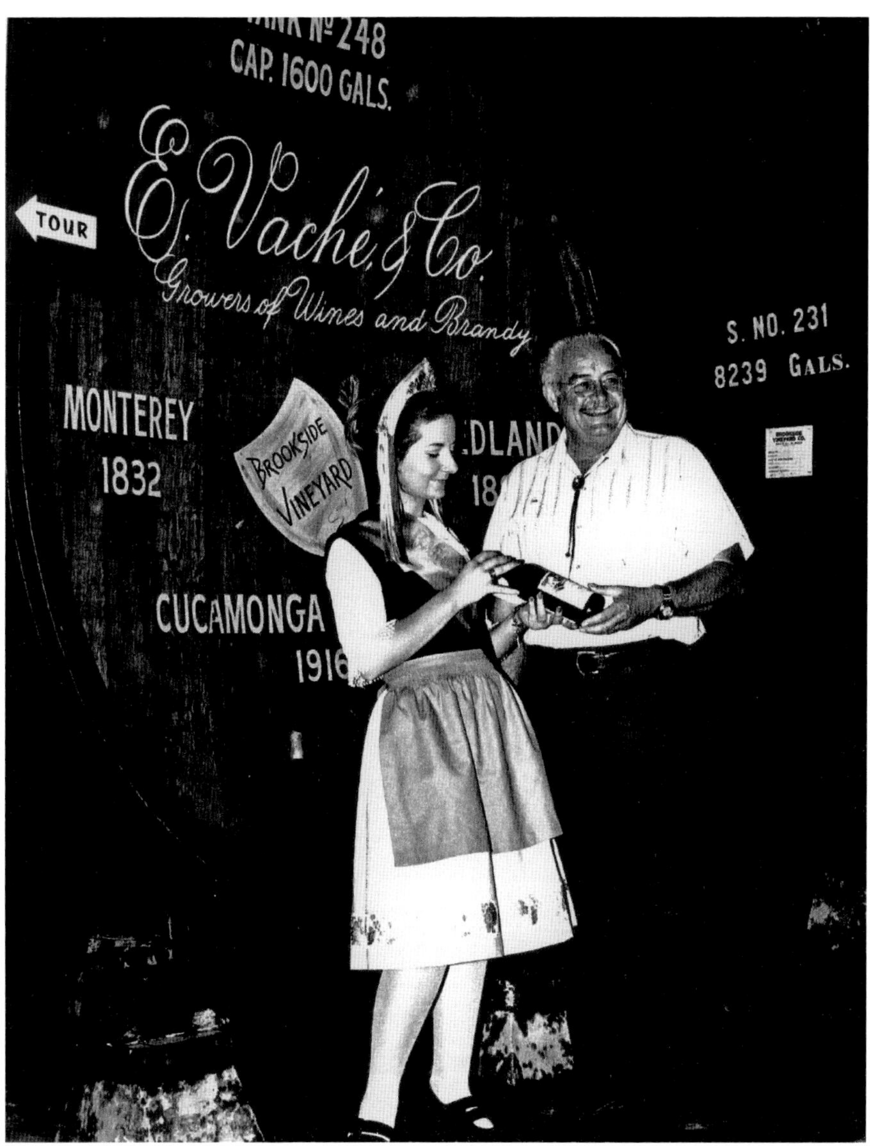

Philo Biane proudly displaying bottle of his wine at Brookside Winery. *Cal Poly Special Collections.*

> *The houses that people lived in were built out of wood. We didn't employ stucco in those days, we just used wood sidings on the houses. The houses were not very sturdy. We still had this pioneer philosophy of being semi-temporary in a location, people always had the thought of moving on to something different. That's the reason they were here in the first place, because they had moved from some place to here. There was no insulation in them at all. The rooms were plastered and they did have wall paper, but that was about as far as it went. The houses were scattered because everybody had quite large land holdings of 40 acres and up, and therefore you didn't have close neighbors. The town of Cucamonga has ten or fifteen houses which were next to one another, the rest were scattered throughout the whole valley.*

Philo took over the operation when Marius passed away. Philo grew the winery with his sons, Michael and Pierre, for twenty-three years. In the 1960s, the winery became the largest winery in Cucamonga, with a storage capacity of 8 million gallons. The Biane brothers were pioneers in off-site tasting rooms, which could be found all over Southern California. At the height of their production, there were thirty-five tasting rooms, some of which were located in Arizona and Illinois.

Brookside winery was bought by Beatrice Foods in 1973, and it continued to make wine for the next ten years. "Beatrice Foods was a large company that was publicly traded on the New York Stock Exchange," Michael Biane explained. "These large types of corporations do not like the cycles of the wine industry. When there are low years, they cannot predict what the next year would bring. This is too risky for shareholders. Coca-Cola once tried their hand in the wine industry, and that only lasted for five or six years."

Family-owned wineries are the only kind that have survived the test of time, and some have been wildly successful. The Gallo wine empire is a good example. They were the first family to become billionaires after income taxes were introduced in America. Prior to that, there were other billionaires, but their fortunes had been untouched by income tax. The Gallo family has continued to grow and prosper, and they understand the ups and downs of the wine industry and have survived because of their multiple generations of experience and knowledge.

Beatrice Foods did not have the patience to continue in the wine industry and liquidated Brookside after ten years. It made a fortune from the deal because when it bought Brookside, it also acquired its land assets and made a tidy profit from selling the hundreds of acres of land to developers.

BROOKSIDE WINES

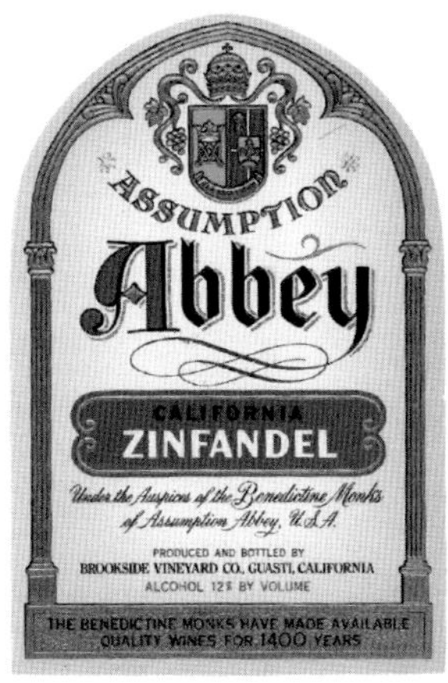

Wine bottle label from Assumption Abbey Zinfandel Wine, produced at Brookside Winery. *Cal Poly Special Collections.*

Brookside was known for its table wines and Zinfandel, as well was dry and sweet vermouth. It also had E. Vache, which was a subsidiary brand. Brookside also produced altar wines, notably its Assumption Abbey Zinfandel Wine. This was produced through an arrangement with the Benedictine monks of Assumption Abbey in Richardton, North Dakota. The monks wished to bring their old-world tradition of producing wine to a modern market. This led to the creation of the Assumption Abbey Winery, which did business under the Brookside Winery business.

The Benedictine monks had a tradition of winemaking that spanned more than 1,400 years, and Abbot Hunkler, who was the abbot of the Assumption Abbey at the time the wine began to be produced through Brookside, was known as the "Wine Abbot." The new Assumption Abbey wine was distributed throughout California and all the way east to New York, with many points in between. The wines sold under this label included:

REDS
- Cabernet
- Dido Noir
- Zinfandel

WHITES
- St. Emillon Vertdoux Blanc

ROSE
- Vin

DESSERT AND APERITIF
- Tinta Port
- Sherry Palido
- Sherry De Oro

- Sherry Crema
- Cream Marsala
- Cream Muscat

Champagnes

- Brut
- Extra Dry

In the tradition of Brookside Winery, Assumption Abbey wine also produced altar wines for clergy.

In 1969, Brookside Winery acquired the twelve Mills Winery roadside cellars in Northern California. Along with the sixteen cellars the Biane family already owned, it became the largest direct-to-consumer winery company in the country.

In 1972, Philo retired, and his son Pierre took over operations. Philo's son Michael went into the real estate business. Philo could not stay away from wine entirely in his retirement and began to produce an Oloroso type of sherry at a small winery that became Rancho de Philo.

Padre Winery

Padre Winery's origins date back as early as 1870, when it operated as the Cucamonga Vintage Winery. In 1909, it was purchased and rebuilt by the Vai family and operated as the Padre Winery, thriving by producing wine and shipping wine grapes to the eastern United States. After James Vai passed away, his widow took over as president of the company, and Promo Scorsatto became the winemaker. It produced table wines, aperitifs, dessert wines, sparkling wines and brandy.

The Padre Winery was one of the few California wineries operating both before and during the Prohibition era, receiving the first federal liquor bond in the state to produce sacramental wines for the Catholic Church. Under new ownership, the winery also produced an "elixir" between 1930 and the end of Prohibition in 1933—in truth, it was liquor that was marketed to doctors and hospitals as a medicinal tonic. Anyone could come in and get a medicinal sherry or port for their "shaking hands."

The Vai family formed the Medicinal Wine Company of California, and during a time when many wineries were closing their doors forever and during the beginning of the Great Depression, the Vai brothers became very wealthy. They were producing five thousand cases of wine and port per day and were making between $600,000 and $700,000 per month during Prohibition. They used the money to develop many areas around the Cucamonga Valley.

Land was cheap, about one dollar per acre, and the Gallos had not started their operations. The complex included two main winery buildings that housed a distillery, a crush room, warehouses, outbuildings and a winemaker's residence. The primary winery structure included a Vermouth dry wine room, cellars, a bottling area, a champagne vault and a fermenting room. The name eventually became Cucamonga Vineyard Company. It became California's Bonded Winery no. 1 after Prohibition was repealed. It gave the wine industry a rebirth in America. It was a fully functional winery during a time when other wineries were trying to get restarted.

SURVIVAL

"You can grow grapes, make wine, but if you don't have a marketing plan, you will fail," said Pierre Biane. The Bianes learned that they had to diversify and be clever in order survive for many years in the wine industry. "Do you know how you can make a small fortune in the wine industry? Start with a large fortune and by the time you finish, you will be reduced to a small fortune," Pierre would often joke. Working at vineyards was difficult, often profitless work.

"I would work 4,000 acres just to break even and be able to keep my family going," said Pierre. When Pierre and his brother were growing up, there were only forty to fifty wineries in the state. Everyone knew everyone. They knew when someone was going to have a baby, and they knew when someone was divorcing. While the industry is a competitive one, they all knew they were in it together.

One of the families the Bianes had dealings with over the years were the Gallos. They have a high respect for the family, even though they, along with other companies such as Franzia, had taken control of the wine industry and now dominate it. "We relied on the Gallo company to buy our grapes and products. It was one of the ways we survived," remarked Pierre.

Gallo would pay the Bianes one dollar per sugar point—that is, the potential sugar in the grapes in the fields. This determined the potential alcohol fermenting the grape juice could produce. "I don't know how we made it. They paid us twenty-two dollars a ton, but it cost us twenty dollars a ton to pick. Can you imagine a profit margin like that?" Pierre said.

The Bianes sold wine in Europe, especially champagne in Berlin after World War II. They produced champagne in their Padre facility and figured out a way to sell it in bulk rather than one bottle at a time. The champagne was sold for $6 per bottle or $30 for a case of six bottles. This was during a time when champagne was selling for $100 from countries such as France. The Bianes used their name (which was French) on their bottles and sold them to people who did not want one bottle but rather wanted to buy cases of wine for celebrations such as weddings. They made it affordable and sold many cases.

When the cases were returned to the United States, they did not let the opportunity pass and just return them empty—they filled the cases with first-run wines from Europe that were highly prized in the United States. The Bianes would sell those wines for $600 per case to casinos in Las Vegas, where they had struck another deal. They sold cases of champagne to all the different casinos on the strip, each with a personalized label. They sold them for $16 per case, and they were used in the casino hotels, which placed a bottle of the champagne in every room, free of charge for the guests. It was a break-even deal for the $16 because it cost them $8 for the glass and $8.86 in taxes. Where they were really making their money was $600 per case in wine that the casinos were giving only to their high rollers. They were selling seven thousand cases of the expensive wine per month. It was all about the volume of sales rather than concentrating on expensive individual sales.

The Bianes would fill their 600,000-gallon tanks with wine and fortify it so that the wine product was 16 percent alcohol and 16 percent sugar. The stills were creating 200-proof alcohol in order to arrest fermentation. The process would take three to four hours before it would be ready to send to Gallo. There would be eight railcars that would arrive every eight hours to ship the wine, and once all of the wine was gone, around Thanksgiving, it was time to crush the grapes and start the process again. Gallo would then take the wine product and use it for the different wine products it produced. This was one of the main sources of income for the Bianes in addition to making their own wine under their own label.

"The Gallos beat all of the other wineries in California because they could produce a lot of wine, and they also created a new type of wine that set them on top: Thunderbird," laughed Pierre Biane. Gallo already controlled much of the distribution in the East, and it also controlled the Burgundy industry.

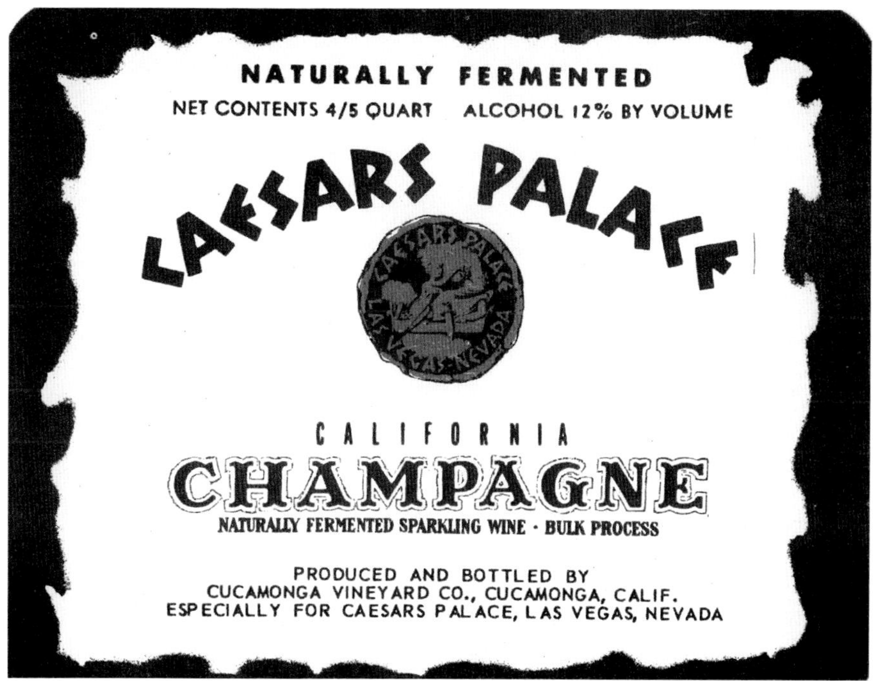

Champagne label produced by Cucamonga Vineyard Company for Caesars Palace Casino and Hotel in Las Vegas. *Cal Poly Special Collections.*

Thunderbird departed from the same type of wine that had been produced for so many years. It was a sweet fortified wine that was targeted at younger generation. This was followed by the Bartles and James line of wines, which were also very popular.

The Biane family learned that in order to survive, they had to look beyond just making and selling wine. They worked at other vineyards in the area. Philo and his brother had been sent back to France for a time during Prohibition to learn the craft of winemaking from professionals. There were no books or colleges that taught the art and science of winemaking in the United States at the time, so they had to study abroad.

Once repeal occurred, the Biane brothers were the most educated people in the area and were sought out for their expertise. Philo taught his sons early how to work in the vineyard. "I grew up with a pair of pruning shears welded to my hand," said Pierre. They would prune other people's vineyards, and they would help make other people's wines. They got into distribution of wines and created retail stores to sell their own wine. Each activity brought them a little bit of income, and with everything combined, it allowed them to make a decent living in the wine industry.

Pierre and Michael graduated from Chaffe College with agricultural degrees. They knew how to grow things, but they were also learning how to sell what they grew. "There are so many great wines out there. Everyone can win a gold medal for their wine, but what does that mean? You can produce a great wine, but without a marketing plan, you will quickly go under," advised Pierre Biane.

They even got into real estate. They would sell properties to investors, plant the fields for free and work those vineyards. Then they would buy the grapes they produced to make wine at the Brookside Winery.

Retail Stores

"We learned that you cannot dictate someone's palate," offered Pierre Biane. Brookside paid attention to what was going on with the Gallo company. It was growing large, and it was pushing other wineries out because it was locking up distribution in areas. Smaller wineries could not compete in supermarkets against the wine giant, and so the Bianes came up with a plan. They opened up thirty-eight retail stores nationwide.

"Look at the different places that sell wine even today. They may sell a few bottles of different kinds of expensive wines, but the companies that are making it have their wine stacked and are selling it by the gallons," explained Pierre Biane. "We could not survive the conventional way; the rules had changed. We could sell ten cases of wine to a restaurant in San Francisco for $1,000 a case. We could be excited that we sold $10,000 worth of wine, but the reality is, the restaurant really will pay for the one case and the other nine cases they expect for free for tasting. So now you are reduced to $100 a case for ten cases. It is not a game you can survive at very long."

They shipped wine by railcar to the various cities, where they sold the wine at retail and would bottle it locally. Each store offered a wide range of wines because they knew if they could just get someone into the store, they could get them to leave with a case of some kind of wine. They offered high-end wines, but their big sellers were the cheaper sweet wines. They used fancy names so that the less savvy buyer would feel like they were buying a higher-end wine for a great bargain. They used names like

Golden Rose (a Muscat wine) and Black Velvet (a Concord grape wine) as a marketing strategy, and it worked. They never charged for wine tastings, so people who claimed that they did not like wine would leave with their arms full of wine they never suspected they would buy.

Between 1937 and 1972, the winery complex underwent ownership changes and significant renovations, including brief ownership by a soda manufacturer. In 1976, vintner Pierre Biane purchased the Padre Winery complex and reintroduced winemaking operations to the facility. The winery complex has served largely as an industrial center since Biane's winemaking operations ceased in 1985. At one point, the complex came up to the chopping block to be turned into bulk storage units. The Bianes held out with the belief that someone someday would take over the complex and repurpose it to be used as a winery once again.

The Padre/Biane Family Winery is now home to Mountain Vista Winery & Vineyards, which opened its doors in the spring of 2017. "We were very excited when we met George Walker and listened to his plans of creating a winery. I believe he has the potential to create a Renaissance of wine in the Cucamonga Region." said Michael Biane.

The Bianes have stayed in the agricultural industry and have their offices in one of the buildings in the old Padre wine complex. They grow carrots, potatoes, olives and other produce on land they own in the San Joaquin Valley. "We love to drink wine, and I love winemaking," said Pierre Biane. "When someone asks me what is my favorite wine, I reply that I have not tried a wine yet that I didn't like."

Even though he loves wine, he would not return to it. Pierre Biane believes that the wine industry in Cucamonga is dead because there just isn't any more land to grow grapes like there once was. "It is a big guy's game now. There are a lot of small wineries up and down the coast, but they cannot really compete with Gallo and Franzia. Gallo produces 2 million cases of wine a day and Franzia produces almost 2 million gallons as well. Between the two companies, that is 4 million cases of wine a day. How can you compete with that?"

The smaller vineyards require the same staff, and their overhead is similar. The big difference is that the larger companies can spread the costs over the volume of products they are selling. A winery needs an accountant, winemaker, lawyer and more. In a company like Gallo, the overhead may be only $0.50 per case of wine, where a low-volume winery may have that same overhead cost it $50 per case. "We had a lot of charity organizations ask us for free cases of wines for their events. We wanted to be a part of community, but how could we just give wine away with a large overhead?" said Pierre Biane.

There is an exception to Pierre's philosophy. He believes in the Mountain Vista Winery because it has a strategic plan for growth, unlike much of its competition. He, like his brother, believes that Mountain Vista can once again put Cucamonga back on the map as a respectable wine producing region.

Chapter 7

MIRA LOMA

GALLEANO WINERY

Mira Loma is located within the district of Jurupa within Riverside County. Originally, the lands were inhabited by Native American tribes—Serranos, Luisenos, Cupenos, Chemehuevi and the Cahuillas. When Spain began expanding its missions in the area, Jurupa became part of the San Gabriel Mission, and the land was used for grazing by cattle and sheep. When the missions began to be secularized in 1832, Jurupa became one of ranchos that had been granted to Juan Bandini by the governor of Mexico in 1838.

In 1851, Los Angeles County was divided into six townships, one of which was San Bernardino which included Jurupa. By 1882, people had begun to settle in the land that was once Rancho La Jurupa. Finally, in 1890, Duglad McRae established a claim on what is now the Cantu-Galleano Ranch. McRae sold the land to Fred and Arnold Stadler, who were prominent business owners in the area who were growing their holdings.

Residents from the Riverside area were troubled by folks in San Bernardino, so they joined with residents of Temecula and San Jacinto Valleys and petitioned the state to become their own county. On May 9, 1893, they were granted their petition and formed Riverside County.

The first post office was created in the Stadler home in 1896, and the name Stadler was also used as the name of the Salt Lake Railroad station located where the tracks crossed Etiwanda Avenue.

In 1900, the Stadler brothers formed a partnership with Charles Stearns and his son, who were Los Angeles wine merchants. Two thousand acres

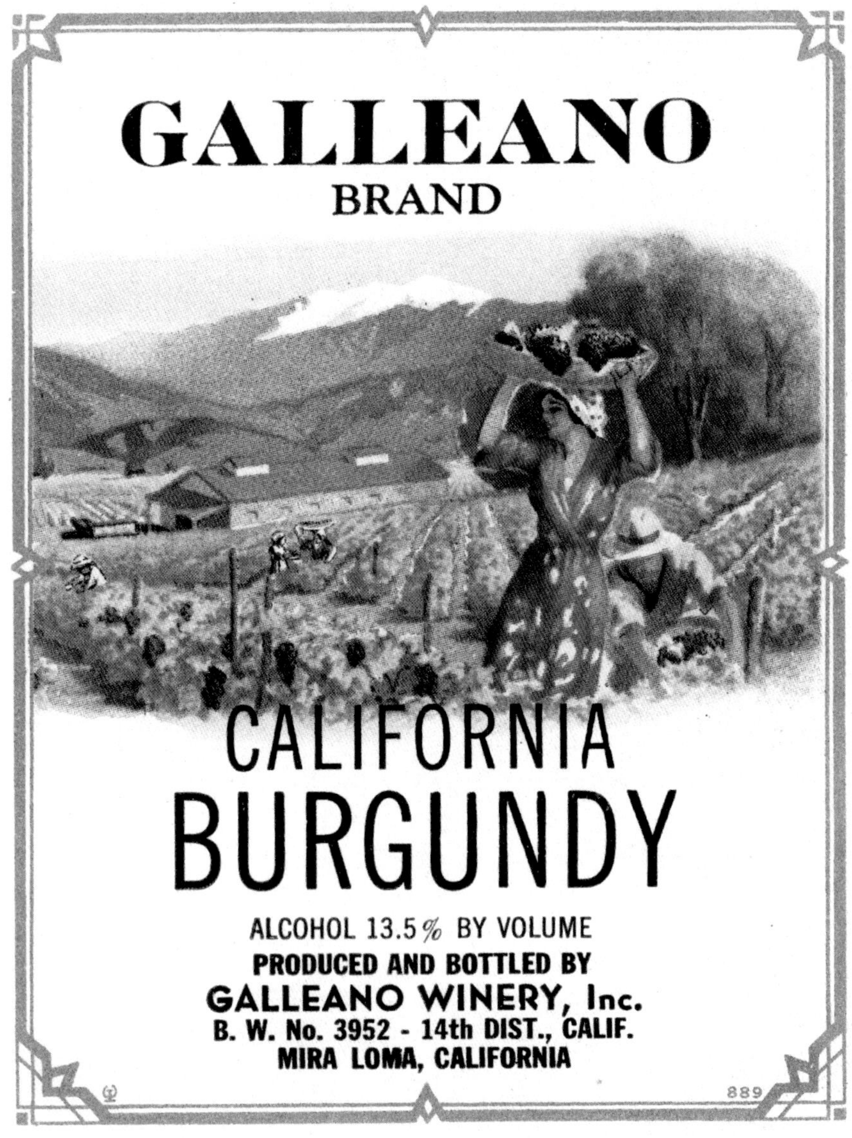

The Galleano Winery still produces award-winning wines, sherry and port produced from some of the few remaining vineyards in what is now known as the Cucamonga Valley AVA. *Cal Poly Special Collections.*

of grapes were planted in Mira Loma, and a winery was born. In 1907, a train wreck was blamed on the name confusion related to Stadler station. There was another station on the same line named Streeter, and so there was a mix-up in train orders. In order to prevent another catastrophe in the future, the railroad station and the post office were renamed Wineville because of the thriving wine industry growing there. The name unfortunately became synonymous with one of the most infamous serial killings in California history.

THE CHICKEN COOP MURDERS

In 1926, Sanford Clark, a fifteen-year-old, had been taken from his home in Saskatchewan, Canada, by his twenty-one-year-old uncle, Gordon Stewart Northcott, to live on a farm with his mother in Wineville. Clark's sister, Jesse, who was nineteen at the time, once visited her brother. After Jesse returned home to Canada, she reported to the American consul that she was very concerned about her brother's well-being.

Authorities at the Los Angeles Police Department were notified, and the department notified the United States Immigration Office. U.S. immigration inspectors Judson F. Shaw and George Scallorn went to the farm to find Clark and take him into custody. Northcott and his mother saw the inspectors driving up to the road and told Clark to lie and delay them while he and his mother escaped. Clark told the agents that his uncle and grandmother, Sarah Louise, were not there; meanwhile, the two fugitives ran through the woods that surrounded their chicken farm.

Clark finally felt comfortable enough to tell the agents the truth about where they were and the story of the horrors he had experienced while in their care. A manhunt eventually caught up with Northcott and Sarah Louise near Mount Vernon, British Columbia, a few weeks later.

Clark testified about the deaths of four boys who had been abducted and abused by Northcott and his mother. The shallow graves of three of the boys were found by the authorities on the property. They contained fifty-one anatomical human parts. These were the bodies of three missing children: Walter Collins and Lewis and Nelson Winslow.

The Clint Eastwood movie *The Changeling* was based on the story of Walter Collins. Walter, age nine, was abducted on March 10, 1928, from his Lincoln Heights home. At first, Christine Collins, his mother, believed it was enemies of Walter's father, Walter Collins Sr., who was an inmate at Folsom State Prison for eight armed robberies.

The story of the disappearance spread nationwide, and the Los Angeles Police Department was soon overrun with leads. Five months later, the department thought that it had caught a break when a homeless boy in Dekalb, Illinois, claimed to be Walter Collins. Christine paid for the boy to be sent back to California, and the department quickly announced that the case was closed. When the boy arrived, Christine knew that something was wrong—this was not her son. This was not good news for the police department, as they had received a lot of bad press and public pressure due to the case. When Christine insisted that the boy was not hers, the police captain, J.J. Jones, told her to take the boy home and "try him out for a couple of weeks."

Christine returned three weeks later, still insisting that the boy was not Walter. She even had dental records to prove it, but Captain Jones would not listen and had her committed for a psychiatric assessment. While she was incarcerated, the police chief questioned the boy, and he admitted that his name was Arthur Hutchins Jr. and that he had run away from his home in Iowa. Christine was released and sued Captain Jones for $10,800, which he never paid.

The Winslow brothers—Lewis, age twelve, and Nelson, age ten—were abducted on March 16, 1928, on their way home from a yacht club meeting in Pomona, California. Once Northcott went to trial, Nelson Winslow Sr., the boys' father, formed a lynch mob to get Northcott out of jail and hang him. The police broke up the crowd before it could get to Northcott.

The fourth victim Clark testified to was a Mexican boy whom Northcott had killed and forced Clark to bury (the head) in a fire pit; the body was left on the side of the road near La Puente, California. Northcott was admitted to killing at least five boys, but some believe that he may have killed as many as twenty. He was convicted of the murder of the Mexican boy and the Winslow brothers and was hanged on October 2, 1930, at San Quentin State Prison. Sarah Northcott was sentenced to twelve years and was released on parole.

Because of the nationwide attention and the negative press Wineville received, it was decided that the name of the town needed to be changed. On September 10, 1930, the name of the post office was changed to Mira Loma ("view of the hills").

The Winery

The Galleano Winery still exists much as it has since 1927. The Galleano Winery District is the only remaining example of a bonded Prohibition era winery that is still owned and operated by the original family in its original location.

The founder of Galleano winery was Domenico Galleano, who was born on October 17, 1888, in Benevegienne, Italy, to Bernado and Maddalena. Domenico had seven brothers and sisters, and they were raised in Magliano Alpi, in the Northern Piedmont region of Italy.

In 1906, Domenico took a trip to the United States but returned to Italy the next year and joined the Italian army, in which he served for four years. On March 8, 1913, he married Lucia Blengino, and fifteen days later, his brother Giovanni and his bride traveled to the United States. They connected with Domenico's older brother Angelo, who lived in Huntington Park, California.

The three brothers dry-farmed and sold their crops on the roadside and to locals. Finally, in 1918, in a partnership with the Bora family, they bought the three-hundred-acre Bonita Ranch, which was located on Archibald Avenue south of Riverside Drive. (This is now part of Ontario, California.)

Domenico's younger brother attempted to come into the United States through Mexico, but there was a cap on Italian immigrants. Domenico could see what was going on with Prohibition, and so he went to Mexico and joined his brother and they opened a distillery in Tecate, Mexico. They produced spirits and waited out Prohibition until 1925, when they became nationalized in Mexico.

In 1915, Domenico met and befriended Colonel Esteban Cantu, who served as the territorial governor of Baja California from 1915 to 1921. Cantu was on the wrong side of the conflict in Mexico and was a supporter of Pancho Villa in the Mexican Revolution. Things became tenuous for Cantu, so he sought political asylum in the United States. He established a home and ranch in Mira Loma.

The political climate began to settle in Mexico, and Cantu returned to Mexico as the first senator of Baja California. He owed Domenico $40,000 from their time together in Mexico, so it was time to return the favor. In 1927, Domenico was given the 160-acre Cantu Ranch in the Wineville area of the Cucamonga Valley and created their own winery. The property had a house, barn, outbuildings and a vineyard. Domenico, Lucia and their children Bernard, Nino and Maddalena worked hard to remodel, plant more vineyards and create a space for wine storage. They began making wine in their basement with just the basics. The remodeling was completed in 1931. All of this was occurred during Prohibition, which was not repealed until 1933.

During Prohibition, like many of the vineyards in the area, the Galleanos sold grapes for home winemaking and were able to open up the vineyard in earnest in 1933. They did produce wine between 1927 and 1933, but it was only for personal consumption.

As mentioned earlier, the area used many workers through the Bracero Program, which was composed of Mexican labor. The Galleanos built

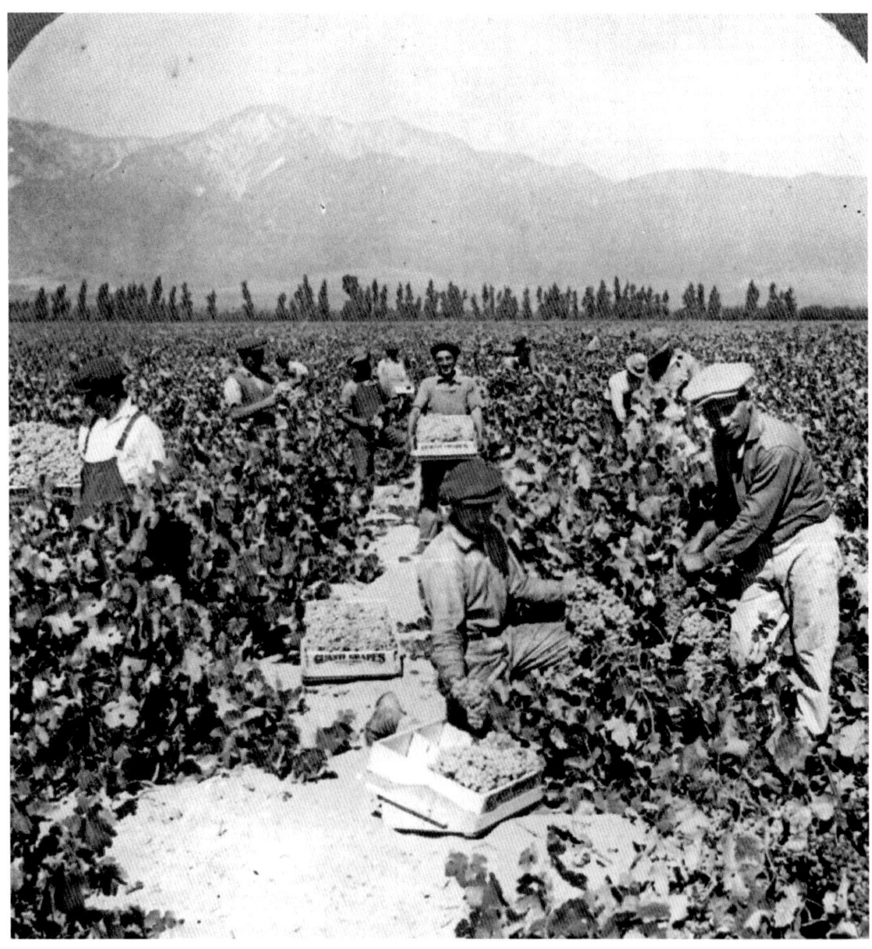

Picking and packing Malaga grapes at the five-thousand-acre vineyard in Guasti. *Cal Poly Special Collections.*

small bunkhouses to house the workers, especially during the grueling harvest months. The Italian and Mexican cultures shared much of the same religious ideology, and the families became close and created an atmosphere of cooperation and cohesiveness.

In 1933, the winery opened up its doors in one of the outbuildings on the property, and the basement served as a storage area for between seven and eight thousand gallons of wine. The family expanded their vineyard and included Zinfandel, Grenache, Mourvedre, Muscat of Alexandria, Burger and, of course, Mission grapes. Because of their growth between 1947 and 1950, a new winemaking facility was built.

In 1952, Donald (Don) Domenic Galleano was born, destined to be a third-generation winemaker, and he still runs the Galleano Winery. Don did not take over the vineyard, so after high school, he moved to Bakersfield, where his father had a farm, and Don began row crop farming. Don was married, and it did not take too long for him to decide to return to the Cantu ranch and take over the business there. He has been the owner ever since.

His son, Domenico Bernard Galleano, does many of the day-to-day operations around the winery and one day will take over the family business. It is unusual because many of the family wineries vanished when younger generations no longer wanted to farm and live the difficult life of a vineyard owner. The family still owns three hundred acres of vineyard spread over the region and employs about a dozen workers. They harvest from some of the same Zinfandel grapevines that Domenico had planted in the 1920s. They also grow some Grenache. They have a close relationship with the Bianes and make port and sherry with the Biane family the same way they always have.

Little Domenic has dreams of expanding and updating the winery, but he knows that the urban sprawl will not abate. During an interview, Dominic pointed at the highway that beyond the vineyard. "You know what people see when they drive past the vineyard? They don't see grapes and history—they just see land that can be developed."

Chapter 8

ELLENA BROTHERS

REGINA WINERY

In 1901, Claudio Ellena came to America from Australia, seeking a new life and a place to build a vineyard. He was of Swiss descent, and when he came to Cucamonga and saw the sunny foothills under the San Gabriel Mountains, he knew that, like Guasti, he had found the right place. It reminded him of areas in southern Europe where some of the world's finest wines were produced, as this is where Claudio's family had produced wines for many generations.

In 1906, Claudio settled in Etiwanda and opened up a winery located just a few miles northeast of Cucamonga. Claudio's sons John B. and Frank took over the winery after their father passed away. Their two other brothers were also involved in the day-to-day operations. Arnold Ellena was their winemaker and chemist, and Louis Ellena was their master distiller.

They operated under the Regina brand and produced about 500,000 gallons of wine a year, of which two-thirds were sweet wines:

Red

- Chianti
- Barbera
- Grignolino
- Zinfandel
- Burgundy
- Claret
- Vino Buon Gusto

WHITE
- Sauterne
- Chablis
- Rhine Wine

ROSE
- Vin Rose (made with 100 percent Grignolino grapes)

SWEET WINES
- Natural Muscat
- Red Grape Wine Blend
- White Grape Wine Blend

APERITIF AND DESSERT WINE
- Pale Dry Sherry
- Sherry
- Port
- Muscatel
- Tokay
- White Port
- Angelica
- Dry and Sweet Vermouth

SPARKLING WINES
- Regina Champagne
- Sparkling Burgundy
- Wedding Party Pink Champagne

They also had a wine vinegar plant and sold vinegar at their tasting room. There was a delicatessen attached to the tasting room. The wines produced under the Regina label were bottled in distinctive squat or long-necked containers. Another distinctive aspect of the winery was its mini stallions. It had a team of miniature horses, referred to as "Regina's Lilliputian Horses," that pulled a scaled stage coach. They could be seen daily at the winery and at special events and parades in the area, such as the Rose Parade in Pasadena, the National Orange Show in San Bernardino and the California State Show in Sacramento.

The horses were from Argentina and were twenty-seven inches high and weighed only between 80 and 135 pounds. John Aleno sold the Ellena brothers the horses in 1962. These were Falabella miniature horses, and many of the miniature horses today are descendants of those original twelve stallions. One in particular, named "Chianti," can be found on pedigree papers of many of the miniature horses in existence.

There was also a restaurant at the winery, which was the first winery approved by the governor of California to sell wine made by a wine producer for consumption on premises in 1967. John Ellena sometimes flew his plane over the Cucamonga countryside, and he could see the need for unity among the grape growers in the region. He led a group of them to develop the Wine Advisory Board.

In 1973, the winery was in decline, and it began selling off parts of the winery equipment along with the miniature horses. The site is now leased by the J. Filippi Winery via the City of Rancho Cucamonga.

Filippi Winery

Giovanni Filippi and his son came to California in 1920 from their home in the Veneto region in Northern Italy. The original Joseph Filippi winery was established near Etiwanda Avenue and had 350 acres of grapes in 1922. It grew Palomino, Grenache, Salvador, Mission and Golden Chasselas grapes. It was able to press sixty to one hundred tons of grapes a day when it was in full production. At one time, it had eight tasting rooms around Southern California.

In 1994, it took over the Ellena brothers' winery and has revitalized the facility and continued to plant new vines around the area. Like so many other vineyard owners in the Cucamonga Valley, the Filippi family sold the original J. Filippi Winery to land developers in December 1993.

Chapter 9

THE REVITALIZATION

In 1995, a petition to make the Cucamonga Valley an American Viticultural Area (AVA) by the U.S. Department of Treasury was filed by Gino L. Filippi. In part, it was a tribute to all the vintners who had made Cucamonga a wine empire. A group of winemakers did not want the area to be obscured in history. Even in 1995, the vast vineyards that once made up the Cucamonga Valley were covered in asphalt and industrial storage buildings. Only four of the original families remain in the valley—Biane, Filippi, Galleano and Hofer—and there are less than one thousand acres of vineyard that remain.

The Hofer family has been farming in the Cucamonga Valley since 1882. They primarily grew stone fruit trees, but when the government froze the price of peaches, the Hofers dug up their orchards and planted acres of vineyard. The Hofer family were the some of the founders of the Cucamonga Pioneer Vineyard Association, which included twelve local growers. The co-op farmed more than four thousand acres and worked together in producing wine. The Cucamonga Pioneer Vineyard Association had a winery on the east side of Haven Avenue, north of the railroad tracks. It shipped bulk wine and custom bottled wines by railcar and ship.

The name Cucamonga, especially during and following Prohibition, was respected by buyers of wine and grapes in the East, and therefore there were a number of wineries that used "Cucamonga" in their name. People really did not care which particular winery had the name—they were just interested that the wine or grapes came from the area. A wine label was produced for the Cucamonga Pioneer Vineyard Association that read "Pride of Cucamonga."

The Pride of Cucamonga label was also utilized at the J. Filippi Winery from the 1950s to mid-1970s. The label was revived for 2002 Zinfandel and 2004 Syrah releases. Today, the 2005 Hofer Ranch Syrah and 2005 Grenache Noir proudly feature the Pride of Cucamonga brand.

The AVA was a triumph for Cucamonga, as it states that wines with the Cucamonga Valley designation on their label must contain at least 85 percent Cucamonga grapes. "The greatest benefit is more local identity," said Galleano in an interview with the *Los Angeles Times*. "People here need to take pride in the work that has been done, to realize that the people who lived here before literally turned sagebrush and wild country into a cultivated paradise, and they did that with a lot of hard work. I believe the Cucamonga Valley appellation will pay a tribute to those people."

Much of what is left of the Cucamonga vineyards exists in the area of the Lopez Ranch. It was originally planted in 1918 just before Prohibition had begun to take effect. The vineyards exist between the intersection of Highways 15 and 210 between two stores and stretch throughout subdivisions in Fontana and Etiwanda.

Don Galleano is the most recent caretaker of the vineyards, and the land is farmed organically. The caretakers dry-farm it without irrigation, much as it was done in the early twentieth century. Since the vines are older, they still have their roots tapped into water far below the sandy surface. Some of the roots can reach as deep as thirty feet.

Geyser Peak Winery, Bonded Winery no. 29, exists in Healdsburg, California, and for a number of years produced wines using Cucamonga grapes. The Galleanos only produce about thirty thousand cases of wine now, and so many thousands of gallons of the locally made wine goes to other wine companies such as Gallo and Ravenswood.

RANCHO DE PHILO

Even after Philo's death in 1999, his daughter and son-in-law, Alan and Janine Tibbets, continued to open the Rancho de Philo once a year to sell sherry, which sells out fast. The Biane family has been producing the world-renowned sherry for fifty years. The original winery was opened in 1974 by Philo, even though he had been making the sherry since 1962.

The sherry is made with the original Mission grapes via a process called the solera system, developed in Spain and used to blend different aged wines to the perfect blend.

The grapes are crushed at Galleano's winery, and the juice is then allowed to ferment until it reaches 16 percent alcohol. At this point, grape brandy is added to the wine, which halts fermentation by killing the yeast. The resulting wine is then shipped over to Rancho de Philo and is stored in an insulated tank in which the temperature is raised to 120 degrees. The wine is cooked for several months. Once it starts to turn brown and becomes hazy, it begins turning into sherry.

The newly baked sherry is then put into 150-gallon barrels and left to grow in flavor and complexity for seven to twelve years. Some of the barrels are more than one hundred years old. The sherry is then put into smaller 50-gallon barrels, and then it is blended to the desired taste using other wines of various ages. This process is continued each year so that the sherry is a blend of a sherry aged from twelve to fifty years once it is bottled. Some of the original sherry is blended into each sherry. The resulting sherry is contains 18.5 percent alcohol, with 13.5 sugar. It is a very long and expensive process because up to 30 percent of the original wine evaporates during the baking process.

Each year, Rancho de Philo produces about four thousand bottles. Galleano also sells sherry and port from some of the same sherry being produced under its own label and sold throughout the year in its tasting room.

Seventh Generation

Michael, Pierre, Janine and their cousin Rene represent the fifth generation of winemakers in America, and now it is up to the next generation to keep the tradition alive. On July, 3, 2009, Tim Bacino reopened the Brookside Winery in Rancho Santa Fe, California. Bacino is the sixth generation of Vache/Biane and is the son of Rosanne Vache Biane Bacino, who is Pomp's daughter. He had a dream of resurrecting the family winery and is accomplishing it with his wife, Susanne, and their daughter, Gabriella, who is the seventh generation, giving them the idea for the wine label Gen 7.

There is still hope for this lost empire of winemaking as the few families hold on to their traditions and new winemakers with a passion for the area seek to grow new enterprises. "Yes, I think the Rancho Cucamonga area will continue to have grapes for some time because of the nature of the terrain, the climatic conditions, and the living conditions," Philo Baine said hopefully at the end of his interview. "All these things add up to being able to develop a nice way of life. Therefore, I think that vineyards and the wineries down there will continue to go along for quite some time."

BIBLIOGRAPHY

Adamson, Danette Cook. "Oral History Interview with Ed Accomazzo: Cucamonga Winery." Transcript. Cal Poly Special Collections, Pomona, California.

Bartlett, Lanier. "An Immigration in the Land of Opportunity: The Story of an Italian Who Has Planted in a Desert the Largest Vineyard in the World and Made the Vines Grow without Irrigation." *World's Work* 17 (November 1908–April 1909).

Berger, Dan. "California's Lost Wine Country: Cotes de Cucamonga." *Los Angeles Times*, May 19,1994.

Burnt, Italo. Diary. Cucamonga, 1950.

Byles, Douglass. *Los Angeles Wine: A History from the Mission Era to the Present.* Charleston, SC: The History Press, 2014.

Clucas, Donald L. *Light Over the Mountain: A History of the Rancho Cucamonga Area.* Upland: California Family House, 2002.

Emick, Paula. *Images of America: Old Cucamonga.* Charleston, SC: Arcadia Publishing, 2015.

Galleano, Don. *Early Mira Loma History*. Mira Loma, CA: Galleano Winery, 2016.

———. *The Historic Galleano Winery: Cucamonga Valley's Historic Landmark Winery*. Mira Loma, CA: Galleano Winery, 2016.

Guinn, James Miller. *A History of California and an Extended History of Los Angeles and Environs.* Biographical Vol. 2. Los Angeles, CA: Historic Record Company, 1915.

Mellon, Knox, and Allene Archibald. *Oral History Project: Phase I, Citrus and Viticulture, 1991–1992.* Rancho Cucamonga, CA: City of Rancho Cucamonga Planning Department, 1992.

Melville, John. *Guide to California Wines.* 4th ed. N.p.: Dutton Adult, 1976.

Pinney, Thomas. *A History of Wine in America: From the Beginnings to Prohibition.* Berkeley: University of California Press, 1989.

———. "Wine in Southern California." Essay from the Wines and Vines of the Inland Valley exhibit and program inaugurating the Southern California Wine and Wine Industry Collection, Cal Poly Pomona University Library, October 1998.

Stumpf, Marcia. *Growing up in Guasti.* Guasti, CA, 1999.

ABOUT THE AUTHORS

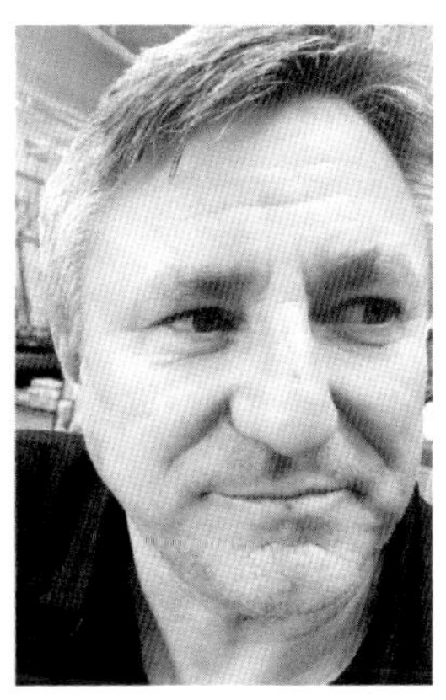

George M. Walker is a native of Peru, Indiana, and relocated to the historic area of Rancho Cucamonga, California, in 2000. With his wife of twenty-six years, Angela, and their four children—Clayton, Donovan, Myra and Ella—George's extreme passion for vineyards and wine has grown exponentially with each year following the making of his first home vintage in Indiana in 1994. His love of the Cucamonga history and heritage is evidenced by the writing of this book and his recent founding of a new "old" winery now located in the same historic facility that once held the Vai Brothers Winery in Rancho Cucamonga.

John Peragine is a published author of twelve books, has ghostwritten many others and does freelance work for the *New York Times*, Reuters and Bloomberg News. He has published articles in *Writer's Digest*, *WineMaker* magazine and *Speaker* magazine to just name a few. John has been writing professionally since 2007, after working thirteen years in social work and as a professional musician in the Western Piedmont Symphony. John lives with his wife and two children in Davenport, Iowa, overlooking the Mississippi River.

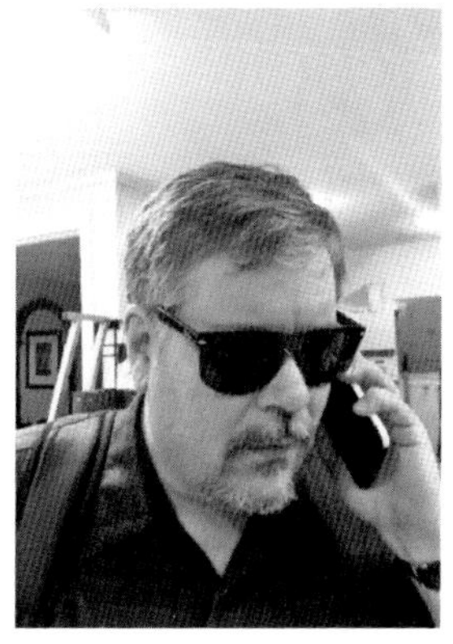

In appreciation for their financial support that helped make this book possible:

Richard and Yan Sum Alvarado	San Antonio Heights Vineyard Estate, San Antonio Heights, CA
Art and Bridget Andres	Snow Drop Vineyard, Rancho Cucamonga, CA
Gary and Connie Andrews	Andrews Inc. Clothing, Glendora, CA
Ryan and Denise Beck	Ryan Beck Photo, Rancho Cucamonga, CA
Brett and Lucy Bender	Bender Estate Vineyard, Rancho Cucamonga CA
Mark Bianco	LaVerne, CA
Danny and Karen Bock	Bock Estate Vineyards, Rancho Cucamonga, CA
Tim and Ina Brown	Rancho Tres Perros Winery and Vineyards, Rancho Cucamonga, CA
Dennis and Patricia Dascanio	Dascanio Estate Vineyard, Fullerton, CA
Michael and Revona Delmedico	Huntington Beach, CA
Gregory and Esther Doonan and family	In Loving Memory of Mateo Sanchez, fifty-plus years working the Cucamonga Vineyards
Dale Erickson	Erickson Estate Vineyard, Rancho Cucamonga, CA
Paulden and Joni Evans	Victoria Hill Vineyard, Riverside, CA
Mark and Marlene Fowler	Fowler Estate Vineyard, Villa Park, CA
Larry and Debby Gott	Long Beach, CA
Kathleen J. Hargrave	Apex Imaging Services, Pomona, CA
William and Nicole Henry	Marriottsville, Maryland
Eric Kaufmann	Pasadena, CA
Dr. Brian and Martha Keyes	Keyes Estate Vineyards, Riverside, CA
Gay and Gina Kuhn	Kuhn Estate Vineyard, Norco, CA
Fred S. Lack III	Lack Estate Vineyard, Rancho Cucamonga, CA
Mountain Vista Winery and Vineyards	Celebrating the Cucamonga Valley History and Heritage
Albert Puglisi	Puglisi Estate Vineyard, Rancho Santa Fe, CA
Kevin and Lisa Rogan	Rogan Estate Vineyard, Upland, CA
Lee and Bonita Roohr	Fontana, CA
Julie Sands	Rancho Cucamonga, CA
Tom and Vicki Solury	In Memory of the Tony and Vera Pizzuto family, Rancho Cucamonga, CA
Ron Stark	Voice Marketing, Rancho Cucamonga, CA
Brian and Patti Stewart	Stewart Estate Vineyards, Glendora, CA
Tom and Debbie Telliard	Telliard Estate Vineyards, Riverside, CA
Corinne Ramirez and Yvonne Trezona	Mountain Vista Winery and Vineyards, Rancho Cucamonga, CA
Eugene and Amanda Verkaik	Beaver Creek Vineyards, Rancho Cucamonga, CA
Charles and Becky Walker	Indianapolis, IN
Clayton G. Walker	MyHomeVineyard.com, Rancho Cucamonga, CA